THRIVING FAITH IN MILITARY LIFE

Copyright © 2021 Planting Roots
All rights reserved.

ISBN-10: 1-7326657-6-1
ISBN-13: 978-1-7326657-6-7
Ebook: 978-1-7326657-7-4

planting roots
STRENGTH TO THRIVE IN MILITARY LIFE

Planting Roots Corporation
P.O. Box 84
Leavenworth, Kansas 66048

All rights reserved. No part of this book may be reproduced, stored in a retrieval system, or transmitted in any form by any means without the prior written permission of the publisher, except for brief quotations of forty words or less.

Unless otherwise noted, all Scripture quotations are from The ESV® Bible (The Holy Bible, English Standard Version®), copyright © 2001 by Crossway, a publishing ministry of Good News Publishers. Used by permission. All rights reserved.

THE HOLY BIBLE, NEW INTERNATIONAL VERSION® NIV®
Copyright © 1973, 1978, 1984 by International Bible Society®
Used by permission. All rights reserved worldwide.

Scripture quotations marked (NLT) are taken from the Holy Bible, New Living Translation, copyright © 1996, 2004, 2007, 2013, 2015 by Tyndale House Foundation. Used by permission of Tyndale House Publishers, Inc., Carol Stream, Illinois 60188.
All rights reserved.

Scripture quotations marked (NASB) are taken from the NEW AMERICAN STANDARD BIBLE®, Copyright © 1960,1962,1963,1968,1971,1972,1973,1975,1977,1995 by The Lockman Foundation. Used by permission.

Scripture quotations marked "MSG" or "The Message" are taken from The Message.
Copyright 1993, 1994, 1995, 1996, 2000, 2001, 2002.
Used by permission of NavPress Publishing Group.

Cover art: Jillian Gilbey
Cover photo: Chantel Jones

Planting Roots is a nonprofit organization encouraging military women to grow in their faith.

This is dedicated to
the women who serve our nation
in the military community:

women in uniform,

wives,

moms,

sisters,

and daughters.

May these words encourage you and strengthen you
so you may flourish wherever your military
journey leads.

Additional Books from Planting Roots

Beyond Brave: Faith to Stand in Military Life
Andrea Plotner, Kindle Direct Publishing (2018)

Free to Be Brave: Moments with God for Military Life
Kindle Direct Publishing (2018)

Bible Boot Camp for Military Women
American Bible Society with Planting Roots (2019)

Flourish Wherever the Military Sends You
Melissa Hicks, Kindle Direct Publishing (2019)

Growing Together: Strength to Persevere in Military Life
Melissa Hicks, Kindle Direct Publishing (2020)

Rise Up: Awaken the Leader Within You
Muriel Gregory, Planting Roots Bible Studies (2021)

More Resources from Planting Roots Authors

Olive Drab POM-Poms
Kori Yates, Crossbooks (2011)

***Holy in the Moment: Simple Ways to Love God
and Enjoy Your Life***
Ginger Harrington, Abingdon Press (2018)

***Journey of a Military Wife series:
Directed: Steps of Peace
Deployed: Steps of Hope
Devoted: Steps of Love
Dedicated: Steps of Faith***
Brenda Pace, American Bible Society (2017)

***Medals Above My Heart:
The Rewards of Being a Military Wife***
Brenda Pace and Carol McGlothlin, B & H Books (2004)

The One Year Yellow Ribbon Devotional:
Take a Stand in Prayer for Our Nation
and Those Who Serve
Brenda Pace and Carol McGlothlin,
Tyndale House Publishers (2008)

Marriage Maintenance for Her:
Tune Up After Time Apart
Liz Giertz, CreateSpace Independent Publishing
Platform (2018)

Marriage Maintenance for Him:
Tune Up After Time Apart
Liz Giertz, CreateSpace Independent Publishing
Platform (2018)

When Marriage Gets Messy:
Overcoming 10 Common Messes Married Couples Make
Liz Giertz, CreateSpace Independent Publishing
Platform (2018)

Blogs from Planting Roots Writers
www.LizGiertz.com
www.GingerHarrington.com
www.KoriYates.com

CONTENTS

Introduction 1

Flourish in . . .

    Abiding 5

    Beginning 11

    Peace 21

    Every Season 27

    Waiting 33

    Intimacy 39

    Friendship 47

    Reconnecting..53

    Building Community 61

    Challenging Relationships.............................. 65

    Separation 71

    Overcoming 77

    Helping 83

    Homecoming 89

    Connecting 95

    Agreement 103

    Teenage Years 109

    Parenting Adults 115

    Loss 121

    Prayer 129

    Praying Like Jesus 135

    Intentional Prayer 141

Ceaseless Prayer 147
Money Matters 153
Saving 159
Teaching Children 165
Not Overspending 171
Moving 177
Residency Change 185
Transition 189
Retirement 195
the Best 201
Hard Work 207
Balance 213
Housework 219
Work 225
Intellectual Health 231
Spiritual Health 237
Frustration 243
Physical Health 249
Remembering 255
Celebration 263
Celebrating Like Jesus 269
Difficult Holidays...275
Identity 281

Conclusion 287
Meet the Contributors 291
About Planting Roots...300

Introduction

By Kori Yates

The righteous flourish like the palm tree,
and grow like a cedar in Lebanon.
They are planted in the house of the LORD;
they flourish in the courts of our God

Psalm 92:12–13

Merriam Webster defines survival as: "The act or fact of living or continuing longer than another person or thing."

In our culture of comparison, this fits right in. If I last longer, if my marriage hangs on, if our kids turn out mostly normal, if I make it to retirement, if I am at least honorably discharged—these are all thoughts that no doubt most of us have entertained at some point or another. Days of counting down a deployment, completing a PCS, or finishing a school year can become days of survival.

God has a much better plan.

John 10:10 says, "The thief comes only to steal and kill and destroy. I came that they may have life and have it abundantly." Abundant life and "just getting by" are not the same thing. Abundant life suggests visions of thriving and flourishing, pictures of hope and joy, and knowing the desire of the Lord for us.

At Planting Roots, we are determined to do more than just survive, we want to flourish. And we want you to flourish as well!

Psalm 92 gives us a picture of a tree that is thriving, growing, and flourishing. Palm trees, in case you haven't noticed, don't usually grow in green pastures or on majestic plains. The tree's roots grow in sandy soil, are flexible and yet amazingly strong. They thrive in areas of low rainfall and last through storms of hurricane force strength. Even after a tsunami, the trees might be gone, but the root ball is still there holding on.

Cedar trees also thrive in arid environments. Their roots go deep into the earth and can soak up almost thirty gallons of water a day from soil that seems totally dry.

Both the palm tree and the cedar tree remind me of military life. The psalmist refers to these trees as examples of the possibilities for those who plant their roots in him.

Introduction

Challenging times often feel like a living in a dry and parched land, a land God knew about before the words of Psalm 92 were ever penned. Military life, and life in general, brings storms, drought, and desert places. We were not made to simply survive, but to flourish in the hard places.

In storms and droughts of work, marriage, children, and community, in duty stations that are hard, lonely, and dry, and in seasons that seem to bring one challenge immediately after another, he made us to flourish regardless of situation or circumstance. He created us to live in abundance.

At Planting Roots, our core verse is Jeremiah 17:8: "He is like a tree planted by the water, that sends its roots out by the stream, and does not fear when heat comes, for its leaves remain green, and is not anxious in the year of drought, for it does not cease to bear fruit."

There's that tree again. Withstanding storms and drought, it finds its source of life, flourishing, in the place where it is.

I want to be that tree.

Don't you? Do you desire to flourish in this military adventure, overflowing with joy and hope into the world around you? To grow in grace, thriving wherever the military sends you? God has great things in store, and we are determined to live a life of abundance. We are determined to flourish.

To do so, we must go back to the source. Together, as we encourage and equip each other in our walks with the Lord, we can grow and thrive in the places where we are found.

I

Flourish in Abiding

By Muriel Gregory

Bloom where you are planted. I remember the first time I saw that saying. We had moved to North Carolina and I was a new bride learning to be a wife—making all the mistakes but trying very hard. An older lady (it is funny now that I would say "older lady" because she was younger than I am now) took me under her wing and spent time with me.

The first time I went to her house, she asked if I wanted tea and I said yes. Being French, I had never heard of iced tea before. I expected the black, hot unsweetened kind and instead was served a sweet, iced version. I drank it anyway, because I was raised to be polite. However, just in case we ever sit down for tea one day, I still prefer the black, unsweetened hot version.

I looked around in her nicely decorated kitchen, and on the windowsill by the sink was a plaque that read: Bloom

Where You Are Planted. I smiled. It had a drawing of three pots with yellow flowers blooming. It was cute, and I liked the sentiment. Growing up as a Navy dependent, I was never planted anywhere. Having married a soldier, the odds of being planted anytime soon seemed unlikely. Maybe that is why the sign spoke to me so powerfully of hope.

For a long time I pondered that idea of blooming wherever I found myself. From that point on in our military life, I resolved to make the best of every duty station, every move, every moment. Even though I had the best intentions to flourish, some moves were excruciating, some duty stations were unpleasant, and there were plenty of gut-wrenching moments.

I learned over time that we never know what the future holds. I also discovered through tears and heartaches that there exists One who holds my future, so I can rest and ABIDE. His name is Jesus, and it is in him that we find our ability to flourish no matter where we are or what we experience.

> *I am the vine; you are the branches. Whoever abides in me and I in him, he it is that bears much fruit, for apart from me you can do nothing* (John 15:5).

The Greek word for abide in this verse is *meno*, and it means to abide, to endure. Endurance encompasses the ability to withstand hardship or adversity and to sustain a prolonged stressful activity, like a marathon. I do not know about you, but at times, military life feels like running a marathon uphill, both ways.

John 15:5 reminds me that apart from Jesus I can do nothing. The only way for me to bloom where I am planted, the only way I can truly flourish is by abiding in him.

How to Flourish by Abiding

1. **What it looks like.** Hold on to his teachings. Obey his teachings. Live like Christ. Join in fellowship with him through communion in the scriptures and with other believers.

2. **How to abide.** Ask for the help of the Holy Spirit as you practice resting in Christ by faith.

3. **What happens.** I am fruitful. My prayers are answered. I have victory over sin. I am confident about where I will spend eternity.

Abiding in Christ is a choice I need to make every day. Every day I choose to read my Bible. Every day I strive to obey God's teachings. Every day I commit to living like Jesus. Every day I want to bloom where I am planted.

How about you? Have you discovered practical ways to abide in Christ? What specific steps will you take this month, this week, today, to bloom where you are planted?

Verses to Consider

Let what you heard from the beginning abide in you. If what you heard from the beginning abides in you, then you too will abide in the Son and in the Father (1 John 2:24).

And I will ask the Father, and he will give you another Helper, to be with you forever, even the Spirit of truth, whom the world cannot receive, because it neither sees him nor knows him. You know him, for he dwells with you and will be in you. (John 14:16–17).

And now, little children, abide in him, so that when he appears we may have confidence and not shrink from him in shame at his coming (1 John 2:28).

Prayer

Lord, thank you for having sent your son to show me the way. Thank you for the Holy Spirit that abides in me. Thank you for the daily guidance toward a life that is flourishing. Amen.

2

Flourish in Beginning

By Katye Riselli

One year we trekked more than 1,500 miles to a colder, seemingly barren terrain. As we traded our shorts and flip-flops for jeans, I mentally rehearsed all the reasons this would be the worst assignment ever.

The base did not have a house available for us. There were no rentals open for several weeks after our "report not later than" date. When my husband checked into TLF (Temporary Lodging Facility), the lodging representative indicated we could only stay for two nights because it was their busy season and they had tourist reservations to honor. We had to stay downtown in a hotel until we found a place to live.

Within forty-eight hours, my husband checked into his new job. Three times over the next ten days I packed our suitcases and moved my two girls between over-priced hotels. Eventually, we received keys to a rental property located right outside the base. We traded two beds in a single room for camping in sleeping bags in an empty house.

As I waited for my household goods to arrive, I longed for a welcoming face to knock on my door. My girls waited for friends. We waited for this new place to feel like home. Nothing we waited and yearned for arrived according to our timeframe.

My thoughts and emotions warred between temper tantrums with God, anger at the military, and resentment for all who had not offered help. Who were these people? Didn't they know the military community is famous for welcoming newcomers? Where were we? Had we discovered the remote outpost for hermits? I missed the familiar and comfortable.

Each morning as my girls and I ate cereal in paper bowls, conversation turned to memories of our last home, the friends we missed, and the community that still held our hearts. That beautiful place had seemed like an oasis, and the stark contrast to our new location broke my heart. It felt like we were exiles in the desert, left to wander alone in silence.

I wore a smile for my family, but I could not wear a brave mask forever. The turmoil in my heart leaked out of my eyes. The thoughts that raced through my mind became words spilling out of my mouth. Whatever we rehearse, we perform. My tiny audience of three took their cues from me. Would we be happy here? The weight of their expectant faces forced me to my knees. *God, are you here in this lonely place? Do I truly believe you go with us and before us into every place you call us?*

I recalled my conversation with a good friend from church right before we moved north. She had asked me to share (on camera) a story about our women's group to encourage other ladies to join. Surprised by her request, I suggested she ask other members who weren't moving, because soon mine would be an unfamiliar face to new women at the church.

"They won't recognize your face, but they'll recognize your story," she said. "Your words will be familiar even if your face isn't, because it's their story, too. We're all newcomers sometimes, somewhere. We all experience being new at some point—we start over—we begin again each January."

As I listened to my civilian friend draw parallels between military life and the life of faith, I began to understand her perspective. The choices I made when we first arrived in that former community created the future conditions for my family and me to flourish in. Because I believed God had gifted us with that assignment, I expected his provision. Because I believed God is the ultimate giver of good gifts, I looked for and discovered his blessings daily. Because I believed God designed me to thrive in community, I sought his people to be my people in this new place. My success in any endeavor—new or old—finds its roots in how I begin.

I stared out at my desolate new landscape and realized the same could be true here. I could continue to lament what I'd lost, resigned to simply survive this assignment, or I could choose to flourish. My choice would set the stage for this new chapter. So, I cued up worship music and blasted truth into my circumstances. As my girls and I sang, I reminded my weary soul of God's character and his faithfulness.

Truth trumped emotion, shifting my perspective and changing the thoughts racing through my mind. Rather than cataloging our frustrations, I counted our blessings— beginning with the fact that we were together in this remote place, rather than my husband being gone and alone on a remote assignment. Even in less than an exotic location, I knew life was better together. The difference between surviving any assignment and flourishing in every assignment is the community.

God always provides me with at least a couple of close friends to be my tribe. Instead of waiting for someone to knock on my door, I called two other new spouses. Before long, we met for coffee and prayer on Friday mornings.

I would love to tell you that desolate barren land became my favorite base, but it didn't. However, it is where I learned to flourish in military life. When I believe God's promises, even the coldest desert can become my promised land. No matter where we go in the future, I know these steps set the stage to flourish in every season of any assignment.

How to Flourish by Beginning

1. **Choose to believe God.** The Lord is the same today, yesterday, and tomorrow. He is always with you. He goes before you, walks beside you, and promises his protection and provision in every place you set your foot.

2. **Choose to be grateful.** Cataloging complaints doesn't change circumstances, but gratitude changes attitudes. Whatever you rehearse in your mind and heart will take life in your words and actions. Flourish by counting your blessings and shifting your perspective.

3. **Choose to be in (or build) community.** Life flourishes in community. We were not meant to do it alone. How can you be part of your local community? If you're lonely and looking for a friend, be the friend you're looking to find. There is always, always, always someone who feels like you. Reach out—you might be a lifeline someone else needs.

Flourish in Beginning

Consider which of these elements of a flourishing life you're missing today. What choices do you need to make to alter the landscape of your life?

No matter where you live, you are here and reading these words because God brought you to this time and space. You are here because God knew what you needed before you had words to articulate it. God knit your heart to desire community, to thrive in community, and to build community. It begins with knowing God, believing him, and choosing to live by faith, fueled by love.

Whatever your goals or dreams, your success grows out of how you begin. Each morning, each Monday, each month—all year long—these beginnings set the stage to flourish.

Verses to Consider

After the death of Moses the servant of the Lord, the Lord said to Joshua son of Nun, Moses' aide: . . . I will give you every place where you set your foot, as I promised Moses. . . . As I was with Moses, so I will be with you; I will never leave you nor forsake you. Have I not commanded you? Be strong and courageous. Do not be afraid; do not be discouraged, for the LORD your God will be with you wherever you go (Josh. 1:1, 3, 5, 9 NIV).

The Lord will guide you always; he will satisfy your needs in a sun-scorched land and will strengthen your frame. You will be like a well-watered garden, like a spring whose waters never fail (Isa. 58:11 NIV).

A good man brings good things out of the good stored up in his heart, and an evil man brings evil things out of the evil stored up in his heart. For the mouth speaks what the heart is full of (Luke 6:45 NIV).

Prayer

Lord, help me set the stage to flourish right now. I want to believe you, God. Help my unbelief. Remind me of your faithfulness. Fill my mind and my heart with your goodness. Amen.

3

Flourish in Peace

By Claudia Duff

For the past few years, encouraged by the book ***One Word that Will Change Your Life***[1], I have chosen a word to focus on for the entire year. My word for this year is *peace.* Past words have been *courage, strength, forgive,* and *brave.* I have waited six years for the word *peace*, and this year it is mine. All mine!

When I hear the word peace I immediately think quiet, solitude, and rest. All these wonderful words take place in an atmosphere of relaxation. Who in their right mind would not want that? I want it, and I long for it right now. After I settled on the word peace, I immediately looked for a Bible verse to focus on to give the word more depth. The Lord led me to this verse: *Turn away from evil and do good; seek peace and pursue it* (Psalm 34:14).

---

1 *One Word that Will Change Your Life*, Wiley Publishing, 2013

Seriously? That's the verse I got for peace? There is nothing restful or even quiet about this verse of Scripture. It's more like a road map for all kinds of shenanigans.

Consider the amount of movement in this verse:

Depart—requires not just movement but direction.

Seek—means I am in a fervent mode of operation. I am not merely looking I am actively searching.

Pursue—yes, I am now in a flat-out chase.

Think about it. When you read these words, you get a sense of urgency that stirs a need to get moving. All of this to say, be careful what you ask for, you just might get it.

So, here I am with my long-awaited word "peace." I'm a bit scared . . . but in a good way. Peace has now become something altogether different for me. It is no longer a place that finds me, but rather a journey where peace is the destination. I am always up for an adventure.

What about you? What are you chasing down right now? It doesn't have to be "one word," it can be a verse, a sentence, or even a book of the Bible. Embrace it and go after it.

How to Flourish in Peace

1. **Daily devotional**. A couple of my favorites include *The Songs of Jesus: A Year of Daily Devotions in the Psalms* by Timothy Keller and *New Morning Mercies: A Daily Gospel Devotional* by Paul Tripp.

2. **War binder.** My personal journal where I write prayers, worship songs, and sermon notes.

3. **Weekly Bible study**. Attend a weekly Bible study at church or in someone's home.

4. **Create a worship playlist.** Put together a playlist of favorite worship songs in iTunes, Spotify, or YouTube.

5. **Daily prayer Alarm.** I have 0700, 1400 and 1600 alarms on my phone to remind me to pray for specific people. The app "Echo" can help with this.

Occasionally I try to mix it up a bit and add some journaling in my Bible that looks more like stamping, coloring, painting, and scrapbooking. In the past few years, I have not done this type of journaling, but I have recently felt the need to color and glue again. So, I am excited about adding that back into the mix.

If you struggle with spending time with God, start slowly until you find your groove. This works for me, the emphasis being on 'me,' my life as it is right now. It didn't always look like this. When my children were young my quiet time lasted about ninety seconds, unless I got up early or stayed up late. God promises to bless and multiply whatever time you offer Him. We serve a gracious God who is for us. As much as you desire time with him, God desires to engage with you even more.

Verses to Consider

You keep him in perfect peace whose mind in stayed on you, because he trusts in you (Isa. 26:3).

For he himself is our peace, who has made us both one and has broken down in the flesh the dividing wall of hostility (Eph. 2:14).

Strive for peace with everyone, and for the holiness without which no one will see the Lord (Heb. 12:14).

Prayer

Lord, although I may fail, I am not a failure. You see me as forgiven and loved. Lord help me to depart from evil and do good. To seek peace and pursue it with my whole heart. Let me remember your forgiveness daily. Amen.

4

Flourish in Every Season

By Brenda Pace

This spring I had the pleasure of leading a women's retreat. I facilitated a session on the topic of "Flourishing in Every Season." The group was a great mix of age, ethnicity, spiritual maturity, roles, stages, and military life experience. I purposely crafted the session to be interactive so I could hear the questions and collective wisdom around the room. I wish you could have heard the lively and meaningful discussion that took place on that sacred ground.

Together we shared the struggles and fears that accompany seasons of transition. Together we looked at the truth found in God's Word and celebrated the discoveries—no matter the age or stage. We found purpose, hope, and victory. I dare you to read the scriptures below and not shout, "Amen!" before you get to the end. Aren't you grateful for the words of hope, wisdom, and truth found in Scripture?

Transitions into new seasons of life are inevitable. The days and years pass—we age, we PCS, we change jobs, we launch children, we walk through sorrow, and we celebrate. The question of the day is, how do we flourish in every season?

When I read the Oxford Dictionary, I know I'm flourishing if I "grow or develop in a vigorous way, especially as the result of a particularly congenial environment."[2] When Uncle Sam is involved in the equation, "congenial environment" doesn't always apply to our experience in the military.

This is the beauty of our counter-cultural, always with us, will work all things for our good God. His definition of flourish is not the same as Oxford's. In God's economy, flourishing is not all about our comfort, ease, or success. Despite our circumstances, we can flourish.

Consider these keys to spiritual flourishing found in Psalm 52:8–9:

> *But I am like a green olive tree in the house of God. I trust in the steadfast love of God forever and ever. I will thank you forever, because you have done it. I will wait for your name, for it is good, In the presence of the godly.*

---

2 "flourish." Oxford Dictionary of English, 3rd ed., Oxford University Press, 2010, p. 672.

Flourish in Every Season

The New English Translation version of Psalm 52:8 reads: *But I am like a flourishing olive tree . . . I continually trust in God's loyal love.* The word "continually" communicates to me that no matter what the season brings, no matter how challenging it may be to adjust, even if it is a season of loss or plenty, I will continually—every day and forever and ever—trust in God.

How to Flourish in Every Season

1. **Trust.** I flourish when I trust in God's steadfast and loyal love—every day in every season.

2. **Thank.** I flourish when I thank God for what he has done for me in the past, knowing he will be faithful in the present and the future.

3. **Wait.** I flourish when I wait on him to fulfill his purpose in each season of life.

Verses to Consider

For the grieving: The Lord is near to the brokenhearted and saves the crushed in spirit (Psa. 34:18).

For the upcoming PCS: The Lord will keep your going out and your coming in from this time forth and forevermore (Psa. 121:8).

For the deployed spouse: I wait for the Lord, my soul waits, and in his word, I hope (Psa. 130:5).

. . . For the retiree: But one thing I do: forgetting what lies behind and straining forward to what lies ahead, I press on toward the goal for the prize of the upward call of God in Christ Jesus (Phil. 3:13b-14).

For the young woman: Let no one despise you for your youth, but set the believers an example in speech, in conduct, in love, in faith, in purity (1 Tim. 4:12).

For the older woman: . . . teach what is good (Titus 2:3).

For the new mom: He will tend his flock like a shepherd; he will gather the lambs in his arms; he will carry them in his bosom, and gently lead those that are with young (Isa. 40:11).

Prayer

Lord, help me to discern your purpose for the season of life in which I find myself. Like the psalmist, *I cry out to God Most High, to God who fulfills his purpose in me* (Psalm 57:2). Amen.

5

Flourish in Waiting

By Jennifer Wake

When I was a little girl, I was sure I would marry someday. Through high school and college, I had many friends, but I didn't date much. Boys were strange. I could understand animals, but boys . . . I couldn't figure boys out at all.

After college, I moved far from my family and friends to become a science teacher in Martinsburg, West Virginia. I didn't know anyone, but in time I made some good friends. *But dating? How does that work?*

I didn't hang out in bars. Churches had mostly older people or people who were already married. Work was full of teenagers and older teachers. I struggled with meeting men. In my mind, the marriage countdown clock started ticking louder and louder. Not wanting to end up alone, I hoped to find the right man to marry. I tried many ways to meet men, but I still could not figure them out.

In that season of my life, it seemed I heard this verse over and over: *Then the Lord God said, 'It is not good that the man should be alone; I will make a helper fit for him'* (Gen. 2:18). In every sermon, even sermons on the book of Revelation, this verse seemed to play on repeat. I felt that God was indicating I needed to marry, so I started adding the word NOW. I needed to marry NOW.

I started praying to marry NOW. I prayed that God would bring my husband soon. I prayed but really it was more like I begged. I begged God for a husband every day and often in the evenings when I was alone. I pleaded with God to take away my loneliness.

Despite my pleading, God remained silent. Instead he worked to change my heart. I was a strong, independent woman who did not like following anyone. Looking back, I realized I was not open to having anyone get to know me deeply.

Instead of a husband, God sent a friend, a spiritual mentor, who encouraged me to follow God. My prayers shifted from seeking a husband to asking God to change me. I prayed for him to transform me to become more like him. I began reading my Bible more and desiring to spend more time at church with people who loved God.

Two years later I moved to Virginia, near Washington, D.C. I shared a house with a group of single Christian girls.

Still desiring a husband, I began to ask rather than beg for the man of my dreams. I assumed a husband would make me feel complete. However, God wanted me to be complete by spending time with him. My memory verse for this season was in James.

> *You ask and do not receive, because you ask wrongly, to spend it on your passions* (James 4:3).

I realized that my passion was to avoid loneliness. I had friends but few knew my heart. Because I did not like being alone, I avoided being alone. Yet God wanted me to spend time getting to know him and being alone allowed me to do that.

Some of the girls I shared the house with were also in their late twenties. We decided to pray for each other for six months and to hold each other accountable in our relationship with God. Studying about loving God more taught me about waiting for true love. We reflected on the book of Psalms which feature many verses about waiting and about longing. As I began desiring time alone with God, I allowed him to fill me and lead me into deeper relationship of love.

How to Flourish in Waiting

1. **Wait with a friend.** Accountability partners or Bible study members can help you learn to grow closer to God. Waiting alone is hard. Ask your friend to check in with a periodic phone call to ask how you are doing. *Wait for the Lord; be strong and let your heart take courage; wait for the Lord!* (Psa. 27:14).

2. **Begin each day in prayer.** Praying while waiting is very important. Starting each day with prayer reminds you who is in control of your life. *O Lord, in the morning, you hear my voice; in the morning I prepare a sacrifice for you and watch* (Psa. 5:3).

3. **Keep serving God.** Complaining doesn't help. I know. I used to lament my single status. God taught that the more I served him the better my days became. *Behold, as the eyes of servants look to the hand of their master, as the eyes of a maidservant to the hand of her mistress, so our eyes look to the Lord our God, till he has mercy upon us* (Psa. 123:2).

I did get married after choosing to wait on God. One of my prayer partners married after I did. Unfortunately, her spouse was abusive, so she is alone again. God has brought her a new way of having a family. As a foster care parent she has a house full of kids, which was her heart's desire. Another prayer partner never married and now works with single women who escape abusive situations. She is serving God by being a role model to these young hurting women. Each of us is flourishing in our own way. None of us are alone because we know God.

Verses to Consider

I wait for the Lord, my soul waits, and in his word I hope (Psa. 130:5).

Be still, and know that I am God. I will be exalted among the nations, I will be exalted in the earth! (Psa. 46:10).

But they who wait for the Lord shall renew their strength; they shall mount up with wings like eagles; they shall run and not be weary; they shall walk and not faint (Isa. 40:31).

Prayer

Lord, please guide me each day to become the woman you want me to be. Guide me in my choice of friends. Teach me to wait on you and your timing. Amen.

6

Flourish in Intimacy

By Muriel Gregory

Okay ladies, it is time for the talk. Yes, that talk. The talk about the birds and the bees. You knew it was coming. How can we discuss flourishing in our marriages without talking about sex?

> *Then the man said, "This at last is bone of my bones and flesh of my flesh; she shall be called Woman, because she was taken out of Man." Therefore a man shall leave his father and his mother and hold fast to his wife, and they shall become one flesh. And the man and his wife were both naked and were not ashamed* (Gen. 2:23–25).

Every time sex comes up in Bible studies or workshops, ladies shift uncomfortably in their chairs. Some stare at their notebooks while others giggle. A handful wish they stayed home.

A gift from God, sex is so much more than the spectacle we have turned it into in our society and even in the church. Biblical sex is intimacy between a husband and wife. Intimacy flourishes within the safe boundaries of a healthy marriage.

> "After the fall, God must have been grieved to see the beauty and holiness of sex turn into the Enemy's playground, to watch it earn a foul reputation, to see what was to be given and enjoyed with selfless abandon between a husband and wife either given away recklessly outside marriage or parceled out selfishly within the marriage."[3]

Both men and women crave intimacy, the place where we feel the most valued and loved. This sacred inner sanctum is where you can be yourself. A place where we freely offer all we are with the person we love the most. In general, men tend to crave physical intimacy whereas women desire emotional intimacy. As your husband provides for your emotional needs, you meet his physical needs.

---

3 Judy Rossi, *Enhancing Your Marriage* (Chatanooga: AMG Publishers, 2004), 35.

After a while, a husband and wife find a rhythm that works for them. Her emotional needs are met and his physical needs are satisfied. However, we know that regularity and routine are not words that accompany military life. We are accustomed to chaos and the unexpected.

When my husband comes home from an extended period away, I want to talk about everything that he has missed. Let's just say that talking is not what he is after. He wants a more physical interaction.

Prolonged separation will break a good rhythm and it can be challenging to find it again. Often this results in one or both partners feeling that their needs have not been met. Communication is the key.

Ephesians 5:22–33 sheds light on healthy marriage:

> *Wives, understand and support your husbands in ways that show your support for Christ. The husband provides leadership to his wife the way Christ does to his church, not by domineering but by cherishing. So just as the church submits to Christ as he exercises such leadership, wives should likewise submit to their husbands.*
>
> *Husbands, go all out in your love for your wives, exactly as Christ did for the church—a love marked*

> *by giving, not getting. Christ's love makes the church whole. His words evoke her beauty. Everything he does and says is designed to bring the best out of her, dressing her in dazzling white silk, radiant with holiness. And that is how husbands ought to love their wives. They're really doing themselves a favor—since they're already "one" in marriage.*
>
> *No one abuses his own body, does he? No, he feeds and pampers it. That's how Christ treats us, the church since we are part of his body. And this is why a man leaves father and mother and cherishes his wife. No longer two, they become "one flesh." This is a huge mystery, and I don't pretend to understand it all. What is clearest to me is the way Christ treats the church. And this provides a good picture of how each husband is to treat his wife, loving himself in loving her, and how each wife is to honor her husband* (Eph. 5:22–33 The Message).

Love and respect are not one sided. They are mutual. Marriages reflect Christ and the Church. It is *give and take*: not an *all take* or an *all give*.

Healthy marital intimacy has been damaged by our culture. Pornography has invaded our computers, cell phones, and TV screens. Reality shows have distorted the beauty of selfless giving as they emphasize reckless entitlement.

Deployments, training exercises, long duty hours, and single parenting are stressors that burden, disrupt, and sometimes destroy the intimate relationship you share with your spouse. Separations because of duty commitments sometimes leads to temptation. Affairs, whether physical or emotional, are not uncommon in our culture. However, there is a way to flourish in intimacy, even in our hectic military environment.

How to Flourish in Intimacy

1. **Strive to be considerate of his needs.** Take the time to find out his love language and do something that will speak love to him. (1 Corinthians 7:3–5)

2. **Respect him.** Respect is earned and respect is due. Ask yourself each morning how you can show him he is important. (Ephesians 5:22)

3. **Communicate often and clearly.** Men cannot read minds. Neither can you. If something is bothering you, communicate it in a calm fashion. Seek to understand and be understood.

4. **Seek help when needed.** All marriages go through rough spots. Getting professional advice will help you identify the issues correctly and provide you with a way forward.

5. **Keep yourself pure.** Jesus tells us that our eyes are the lamp of the body (Matthew 6:22). When our eyes are seeing the right things, our body is filled with light. Beware of what you are watching and reading.

Verses to Ponder

The husband should give to his wife her conjugal rights, and likewise the wife to her husband. For the wife does not have authority over her own body, but the husband does. Likewise the husband does not have authority over his own body, but the wife does (1 Cor. 7:3–4).

Let marriage be held in honor among all, and let the marriage bed be undefiled, for God will judge the sexually immoral and adulterous (Heb. 13:4).

. . . So guard yourselves in your spirit, and let none of you be faithless to the wife of your youth (Mal. 2:15b).

Prayer

Lord, I thank you for the beautiful gift of sex. You created it to be the most intimate relationship between a husband and wife. I pray that my marriage bed will be kept pure and that my union will reflect Christ and the Church. Amen.

7

Flourish in Friendship

By Kori Yates

I went to church one spring morning during my twenties. Not a unique happening in my world, but this Sunday was different. I attended a military chapel where meeting new people is standard. In this setting, people come and go all the time, whether PCS or TDY. We live in an OCONUS (overseas) location, so it takes time to figure out where to plant spiritual roots.

This particular Sunday I met someone new. We chatted about clothes, shoes, and the local stores I frequent. We enjoyed our conversation. As the day went on, our families ended up hanging out together at the local festivities, and then we all went out to dinner. In the course of our conversations throughout the day, she shared the "real story."

This move had been their hardest yet. Many challenges delayed the process of getting settled. Nothing seemed to be going right. Forty-eight hours before, she had been crying, longing to be "back home." A lack of friendly faces made her feel isolated, anxious, and lonely.

Attending church was a place to connect in a new place. The building was not the answer, but the people were. They bravely reached out, praying God would bring them the friends that would make this new place a home. We were thankful to be part of the answer to that prayer.

In Scripture, God reminds us of both the importance of community with him and community with others. He did not make us to live in isolation, but to live a life of abundance and hope with others. In the weariness of starting again, God reminds us of the blessings we have been given along the way and encourages us to find the blessings of the place where we currently find ourselves.

As our family gets ready to PCS again, I remember the challenge of starting over in a new place. For the woman I met at church, our new friendship did not answer all her questions or relieve all her anxiety, but it did remind her that she's not alone. It also made a difference in me because I will soon be the new person. Again.

Scripture tells us to hold on to our hope because he is faithful. We also should not neglect meeting together. I know it requires bravery. Trust me, this introvert gets it.

Our community with God and with others is a necessity for which he made us. We must be intentional—and we won't be sorry we were.

How to Flourish in Military Community

1. **Show up**. Find a local church or Bible study where the Lord would plant you. It may take a few tries but finding the right one is worth it. He has a place for you.

2. **Be brave**. Make the first move. You can start the conversation, ask the questions, and invite a new acquaintance out for coffee.

3. **Remember the blessings.** Remember your friends from all those places before? God has blessed us with friends at every duty assignment. He has given us those with whom we can do life. In remembering what he has already done we can have courage to step out again.

4. **Enjoy community with God**. Building friendships and growing relationships takes time, but there is one relationship that remains constant. Take the time to continue to grow your relationship with God in the season of waiting for human friendships.

God has made us for community. Whether we are headed to a new place or new folks show up in ours—be alert. Watch for those folks God brings across your path to become part of your tribe. He has good stuff in store.

Verses to Consider

And let us consider how to stir up one another to love and good works, not neglecting to meet together, as is the habit of some, but encouraging one another, and all the more as you see the Day drawing near (Heb. 10:24–25).

And they devoted themselves to the apostles' teaching and the fellowship, to the breaking of bread and the prayers (Acts 2:42).

This is my commandment, that you love one another as I have loved you. Greater love has no one than this, that someone lay down his life for his friends (John 15:12–13).

Prayer

Lord, thank you for the friends and community you've provided in the places you have taken me. As I take my next steps, help me to be brave in finding those folks in this new place. Amen.

8

Flourish in Reconnecting

By Claudia Duff

Friends are multiplied in the world of social media. Think about it, who has over 700 friends with whom they should be in daily communication with? Me. So, when people ask to "friend" me on Facebook my immediate response is "Okay, but I am the worst Facebook friend you will ever have."

Don't get me wrong, I love seeing lives unfold before me. Unfortunately, my devotion seems to end there with my 700+ friends. I forget to like, love or be sad at their posts. I miss birthdays like they never happened. I catch what I can, but like I said, I am the worst Facebook friend in the history of Facebook friends.

One morning I reconnected with a dear friend that I hadn't spoken to for three years. You know the drill: she moves. I move. We all move and we often lose touch. Not this friend. She refused to let go, and I am the better for it. Seeing her and sharing a cup of coffee was just what this heart of mine needed most. Hugging, crying, and speaking in fits and starts for a couple of hours rekindled our relationship. Even if only for a couple of hours, we all benefit when we connect (or reconnect) with a friend.

> *As soon as he had finished speaking to Saul, the soul of Jonathan was knit to the soul of David, and Jonathan loved him as his own soul* (1 Samuel 18:1).

My friend and I talked about all the messy things in our lives because our souls are indeed knitted together. We shared our disappointments and the busyness of our lives. We also laughed with deep chuckles about the benefits of knowing our grace-filled God. Giggling like girls, we shared past adventures and caught up on life.

It was good, and it was grand, and it was hard. Sometimes it is difficult to let down your walls and be completely honest with a friend. That day, my friend peered inside my soul when she spoke these words: "How are you? Your face is telling me something's off."

Nope, I couldn't sneak my *everything's-okay-face* past her caring eyes. As I looked, I saw weariness and uncertainty mirrored in her pupils. As believers in a good God who is sovereign over our lives, what are we supposed to do with the hard stuff?

We trust. We have a friend in God who chooses to use us in his work on this earth. I firmly believe we are called to build godly friendships—especially in the midst of hard stuff. We trust God and we pursue healthy and godly friendships. We embrace "iron sharpening iron" and get our swords out! Our God uses us to speak into one another lives, especially in the midst of hard stuff. When life comes at you in harsh ways a battle buddy is needed. Someone who will not just stand with you but actually stand in the gap when you can't stand.

My friend called "out of the blue" right when I was thinking of her. It was a bit unsettling. When you don't speak for many years a phone call seems awkward. But how great is God to have my mind already thinking of her when the phone rang? If you trust him, he will show the same kind of care for you.

Take the first step. Make the first move. Reach out to a friend today.

How to Flourish in Reconnecting

1. **Pray Scripture for friends.** You've heard the saying, "Wild horses couldn't keep them away!" So, for your first step, lock up all your wild horses (scary thoughts) through prayer. Maybe yours tell you something like, *it's been too long*, or *they won't remember me*. Spend time praying for your friend, asking the Holy Spirit to lead you to the perfect opportunity to reach out and reconnect. I keep names of friends in a prayer journal. I also write notes in my Bible with verses marked for friends to inspire encouragement and prayer. This is the first step in reconnecting. The Holy Spirit will guide you in how to pray and when and where to reach out.

2. **Be creative as you initiate reconnecting.** I also love the phrase, "They are thick as thieves." Second step, get the gang back together by planning a time to reconnect. It can be in person, by video chat, or a scheduled phone call. Make sure you can talk as long as you want (like a naptime call). I plan time to regularly connect with four friends even though

we no longer live in the same place. We also share the same devotionals. When someone is having a hard time, we share encouraging verses and resources YouTube worship videos, preaching podcasts, and a gazillion memes.

3. **Protect your friendship.** This is a favorite saying, "you can't squeeze a dime between them." Now that you have reconnected, do not allow time and space to become your dime. Make the effort to stay engaged. Our commitment to interact regularly through messaging, emails and texts has deepened our friendship in spite of the miles that separate us.

Now that you have reconnected, don't let time and space separate you again. The terms, "wild horses, thieves, and dimes," can provide reminders for practical ways of connecting with friends.

Make the effort to stay connected. Not all of us can keep weekly or even monthly commitments but we can dedicate ourselves to some type of resolve to stay in touch.

Some friendships may only last for a season, but others are meant for a lifetime. Friendships are not just for us to take from one another, but to pour into each other. As God fills your heart with friendship, look around and see who is running low and pour it out. Girlfriend, our friends need us.

For the record, my sweet friend and I already have a day scheduled to spend time together. To connect with a friend, it only takes one of you to reach out and one of you to respond. It's not rocket science, but effort is required.

Verses to Consider

But we have this treasure in jars of clay, to show that the surpassing power belongs to God and not to us (2 Cor. 4:7).

A friend loves at all times, and a brother is born for adversity (Prov. 17:17).

And the Scripture was fulfilled that says, "Abraham believed God, and it was counted to him as righteousness"—and he was called a friend of God (James 2:23).

Prayer

Lord, thank you for the gift of friendship. Help me to treat my friends with the love and grace that you give me. I pray that our friendships will deepen and always reflect your glory. Amen.

9

Flourish in Building Community

By Larissa Traquair

I'm an extrovert, and I love being around people. They infuse me with energy that makes everything more fun. Sometimes it is hard to find friends or groups to connect with in the transitions of military life.

When the Marine Corps sent us to Quantico, Virginia, I struggled to find a group to get involved with. Frustration led to inspiration as God stirred me to combine a hobby with building community. Over the years, I have started many crafting groups, and each has been a unique blessing to those who attended.

Building community comes naturally for me but I know that is not the case for everyone. However, you don't have to be an extrovert to make friends, and even a few friends can build a community. God calls us to gather, but it rarely happens by accident.

A healthy community can yield fun, fellowship, growth, and inspiration. Yet, relationships can be messy and frustrating at times. God can help us work through challenges to create fellowship and healthy friendships.

Building community is a chaotic adventure worth the effort to get along. When we keep Jesus at the center of fellowship, we can be patient with one another when relationships don't go smoothly. None of us are perfect, so we should not expect others to be perfect. The benefits of friendship far outweigh the challenges. Enjoying time with the amazing people God puts in your sphere of influence is worth every endeavor we make.

How to Flourish in Building Community

1. **Be unoffendable.** You will not always agree with everyone in your community. You may offend someone at some point. Learn not to take things personally and get comfortable with being uncomfortable as you strive to resolve conflict.

2. **Look to Jesus for your example of doing community well.** Jesus stayed connected to God. We can learn how Christ related to others as we study the Gospel. Jesus knew his purpose and yielded in obedience to God. Every opportunity with others is an opportunity to love and invite them into the blessing of community.

3. **Be the one who invites others.** Initiating relationships can feel risky, but it is worth the effort. Reaching out opens new opportunities to watch community blossom.

4. **Be willing to forgive.** Forgive others who have not invited you or who have hurt you along the way. Even though one military woman hurt your feelings it doesn't mean every military woman is going to hurt you. Forgive and move forward. Don't let a painful experience rob you of the joy of community.

Verses to Consider

For just as the body is one and has many members, and all the members of the body, though many, are one body, so it is with Christ (1 Cor. 12:12).

Bear one another's burdens, and so fulfill the law of Christ (Gal. 6:2).

Put on then, as God's chosen ones, holy and beloved, compassionate hearts, kindness, humility, meekness, and patience, bearing with one another and, if one has a complaint against another, forgiving each other; as the Lord has forgiven you, so you also must forgive (Col. 3:12–13).

Prayer

Lord, thank you for creating us for community and all the benefits of friendship. Thank you for wanting to use me to love others well. Show me who to invite into our community and help me to love them like Jesus. Amen.

10

Flourish in Challenging Relationships

By Muriel Gregory

The room was big and filled with chatter and laughter. The mood was light and festive. From my vantage point I observed all the ladies talking to one another, sharing tips on holiday survival. The buffet was filled with yummy food. Yet I felt like running home and hiding under my covers.

This was my first event for military spouses. Even though we had been stationed at this post for over a year, this was a new unit for us. Relief washed over me as I realized I knew one of the wives in the unit. We had been in the same Bible study together a few months ago and shared many good conversations. We even met for coffee a few times. It is always exciting to see a friendly face in new surroundings.

When I came into the room, I went straight to greet my friend. My smile quickly dissipated as she stared at me, greeted me, and then turned her back to me and continued with her conversation. Wow! That was not what I expected. I felt rejected, left out, and lonely. Feeling isolated in a room full of people can be the most desolate place on earth.

I tried to stick around for a bit, making small talk with a few ladies because I did not want to look defeated. However, my heart was heavy. I just wanted to head back to the safety of my home.

Rejection highlights the worst that has been said or done to me to rob me of my joy. Friendships can sometimes feel like fields full of landmines that are much easier to navigate if you know the location of the mines. Thankfully, we have a guide who has experienced those minefields and can identify with us.

Jesus understands rejection. He knows the pain that envelops you when people who have known you for a long time give you the cold shoulder. Jesus knew that suffering was part of his walk and would be part of ours also. Rejection did not surprise Jesus because he knew it was part of life in this imperfect world. The moment I accepted the possibility of being turned down, it did not hurt me as much.

Too often I assume that every person I meet is a friend. I like to think that every friendship will be full of joy and laughter, and will last forever. However, this isn't always the case.

Another major roadblock in friendships is pride. Both mine and others. Since I cannot change the other person, I need to focus on me and deal with the pride that blinds me. Pride can blind me from seeing another person's point of view. I will also be less likely to forgive trespasses. No lesson will be learned, and no progress will be made without forgiveness.

How to Flourish in Challenging Relationships

1. **Consider what the person may be going through.** There are times when rejection is not geared toward me. The other person can also be dealing with insecurities, challenges, or fears. (Philippians 2:3)

2. **Assume goodwill.** The biggest hindrance in any relationship is communication. It can be easy to make assumptions or jump to false conclusions. When I assume things, I base my beliefs on what I feel is right. However, often what I heard or perceived is not what was said. (Philippians 4:8)

3. **Choose your words wisely.** Regardless of what has been said about me or been done to me, I need to be impeccable in my speech. (Ephesians 4:29)

4. **Remember you belong to God.** I need to always remember to ground my self-worth and identity in God and not in other people. (Colossians 3:1–3)

Verses to Consider

Guard your heart above all else, for it determines the course of your life. Avoid all perverse talk; stay away from corrupt speech. Look straight ahead, and fix your eyes on what lies before you. Mark out a straight path for your feet; stay on the safe path. Don't get sidetracked; keep your feet from following evil (Prov. 4:23–27 NLT).

But first He must suffer many things and be rejected by this generation (Luke 17:25).

Where there is strife, there is pride, but wisdom is found in those who take advice (Prov. 13:10 NIV).

Prayer

Lord, thank you for sending your son. Thank you for knowing the deep pain of rejection and showing me how I should walk. I pray that in all situations I will remain confident that you are there with me, loving me, and guiding me every step of the way. Amen.

11

Flourish in Separation

By Liz Giertz

I am not a patient person. Just ask my kids. Or my husband. Or the cashier at the commissary. Waiting well doesn't come naturally to me. Often, waiting quickly turns to frustration, anger, helplessness, or worry. Sometimes a mix of all the above.

Deployments are a true test of my ability to wait well. During my husband's second deployment to Iraq, emotions threatened to pull me under like a deadly riptide. Every planned phone call that never came. Every news report of a mortar attack in the region. Every change or delay in the timeline. Every homecoming ceremony that wasn't my husband's. Each disaster and disappointment drug me down.

In past deployments I have fixated on frustration and fear. Anger over unmet expectations has ruined days and weeks of my life, as well as the lives of my loved ones. My circumstances have made me feel hopeless. I have been bitter because the people around me didn't or couldn't understand what I was experiencing. Sleepless and lonely nights, intermingled with long and stressful days, made everything seem more difficult.

The turning point was placing my faith in God. Not just in some trite saying, but in the deepest and most personal areas of my life. I came to know he loved me enough to care for me no matter what happened to my husband. I trusted he would never leave me nor forsake me no matter what storms raged around me. I knew he loved my husband even more than I did. And I accepted that he was in control of our destiny. I was incapable of waiting well until I realized it was God on whom I was waiting, not my soldier. When faith finally quieted my fears, I clearly saw the keys to waiting well and flourishing during a deployment. As I looked back on it, I realized the answers had been with me since my own time in uniform.

As a soldier deployed to Bosnia, Kuwait, and Iraq, I knew the people around me were struggling just as I was. Day after day after day, together, we counted down the days until we returned home to our families. We stayed busy and the time passed quickly. Believing in the mission gave us a purpose that made the waiting less pointless. We worked exceptionally hard, but we also never underestimated the value of resting when we could. On some level, we all realized we had never been nor ever would be in control of our destinies or our mortalities.

I discovered these four ways to wait well during a separation and have flourished as I practiced them during each of my husband's subsequent deployments, training exercises, or TDY's. The best part is that these principles work whether you are the one in uniform waiting to come home or the one waiting at home for your soldier to return.

How to Flourish in Separation

1. **Connect with a community.** Having real life people (not just Facebook friends) close enough to provide tangible support takes a load off our shoulders: physically, emotionally, and spiritually. God never intended for us to walk through trouble alone. He provides a community for us and we need to make an effort to connect with it. God is an ever-present help in our times of turmoil (Psalm46:1). He promises to never leave nor forsake us (Deuteronomy 31:6). You can connect with like-minded people at your chapel, a women's Bible study, over produce in the commissary, or on the treadmill.

2. **Pursue a purpose.** Having a purpose that serves others, and ultimately the Lord, helps us see past ourselves and our problems. Survey your community and discover the needs. Where do your own skills and abilities intersect with those needs? Pursuing a purpose makes the waiting meaningful.

3. **Remember to rest.** When we are under stress, our bodies require more rest than usual. However, those

also are times when we are least likely to think about ourselves. I'm not just talking about Netflix and ice cream. I'm talking about soul rest. Sabbath rest. We need to be intentional about carving out time to rest our bodies and our souls to flourish.

4. **Foster your faith.** I cannot stress this enough. Separations bring on many worries and fears that threaten to consume us. I would never have survived on either side of the uniform without my faith. Believing in the God who is in control of the universe, who loves you, and who has your best eternal interest in mind gives you the strength to not only endure deployments, but to flourish during them. Prayer, coupled with reading and meditating on God's Word, are the best ways to foster your faith and to flourish.

We can flourish during deployments and separations by training ourselves to wait well. Ultimately, in any situation where we find ourselves waiting, we can remember that is it the Lord on whom we wait, that he loves us, and is able to make all things work for our good. Even waiting. Ultimately, we all await the return of Jesus and our final homecoming. Let's do it well!

Verses to Consider

And he said to them, "The Sabbath was made for man, not man for the Sabbath" (Mark 2:27).

So, my dear brothers and sisters, be strong and immovable. Always work enthusiastically for the Lord, for you know that nothing you do for the Lord is ever useless (1 Cor. 15:58 NLT).

I waited patiently for the Lord; he inclined to me and heard my cry (Psa. 40:1).

Prayer

Lord, inspire me by your Holy Spirit to wait well. Help me to find a supportive community, to pursue a purpose in serving others, to carve out time to rest both body and soul, and to lean into the faith you have given me. Amen.

12

Flourish in Overcoming

By Muriel Gregory

Preparing for a deployment is hard. The training schedule includes appointments for preparing powers of attorney and the will. Duffle bags, socks, T-shirts, uniforms laid out on the floor. The familiarity of a recent deployment brought me no comfort. As the saying goes, "familiarity breeds contempt." Pre-deployment days brought contempt in my heart. On the calendar, the day he was leaving was circled in red. Time moved quickly, yet it felt as if the days were dragging on. I wanted him to be gone so I could start counting down the days until his return—so I could settle into a new "normal".

I was an emotional wreck the day he left. Promises of letters, care packages, and talks of what we would do when he returned sprinkled our goodbyes. That night I felt emotionally and mentally exhausted. I just wanted to crawl into bed and sleep through the whole deployment and escape the fear, loneliness, and the responsibilities.

The phrase, "Do not be afraid" is repeated many times in the Bible because God understands we are easily frightened. In the English Standard Version translation, 158 verses command us not to fear. The opposite of faith is fear and fear paralyzes. When anxiety becomes my anthem, my faith shrinks.

The root word for fear in Greek is *phobo* from which we get the word phobias. Fear can overwhelm, making us feel helpless.

What are some of my deployment phobias?

- Fear he will not come home.
- Fear he will get injured.
- Fear I will be inadequate with the children.
- Fear he will be gone longer than anticipated.

These are legitimate fears, but they are not reality. Reality is that he is deployed, and I am home waiting. Period. Nothing else.

There are many ways to deal with fear. Since fear tends to isolate, we must be part of a supportive community. God created us to do life with other people. One of the many benefits of community is the ability to communicate with others. Talking through your concerns can diffuse them. When we share our fears, we feel less anxious.

Paying attention to our thoughts and feelings can improve our mental wellbeing. Paul urged us to "destroy arguments and every lofty opinion raised against the knowledge of God and take every thought captive to obey Christ" (2 Corinthians 10:5). God does not want us to live in fear. Mindfulness allows us to entrust our concerns to Jesus and receive his peace.

How to Flourish in Overcoming

1. **Do not isolate.** Seek a supportive community of believers.

2. **Talk through your fears.** Cast away your anxieties.

3. **Be mindful of the present moment.** Tomorrow will be there soon enough.

4. **Have faith.** Faith is the antidote to fear.

I wish I could tell you I never have any anxious thoughts and fear no longer grips my heart, but that would be a lie. What I can tell you is that I am quicker to recognize fearful thoughts and more diligent in giving them to God. My faith has grown stronger since I learned to deal properly with my fears. I may not know what my tomorrow holds, but I know who holds my tomorrow.

Verses to Consider

For God gave us a spirit not of fear but of power and love and self-control (2 Tim. 1:7).

Do not be anxious about anything, but in everything by prayer and supplication with thanksgiving let your requests be made known to God. And the peace of God, which surpasses all understanding, will guard your hearts and your minds in Christ Jesus (Phil. 4:6–7).

Therefore do not be anxious about tomorrow, for tomorrow will be anxious for itself. Sufficient for the day is its own trouble (Matt. 6:34).

Prayer

Lord, I am so thankful that my faith in you is all I need to cast away fear. I am grateful that you will never leave me nor forsake me. Even in my darkest days you are my rock and my salvation. Amen.

13

Flourish in Helping Others During Deployment

By Brenda Pace

A military wife's concern for a husband deployed with a combat unit can be overwhelming. When I watched the movie *Indivisible* based on real life Army Chaplain Darren Turner and his wife Heather. In one scene Heather sees another young military wife sitting alone on a bench. She introduces herself to Amanda and starts a conversation in which they realize both of their husbands are deployed. Heather identifies with and shares Amanda's deployment frustration when she says, "I don't know about you, but this is by far the hardest thing I've ever done."

Oh, that every deployed wife would have a woman like Heather to come alongside and say, "It's okay to feel overwhelmed." Even better if that woman follows those words with, "You're not the only one who feels that way."

Amanda's relief is visible in this scene as Heather gives her permission to acknowledge the feelings of isolation that often accompany military family separation.

Amanda's and Heather's husbands are the ones deployed, but these women express their own sense of feeling battle-weary. Their weariness does not come from combat but from lack of sleep because of a crying baby, anxiety for a husband in a danger zone, and the responsibility of caring for the home alone. The struggle is beyond real.

Military wives become independent and self-reliant out of necessity and experience. The tendency to think, *I have to be strong for others and do things for myself*, can lead to hiding insecurities. If these feelings are not acknowledged, they can result in loneliness, exhaustion, and depression. Heather could have ignored Amanda sitting alone on a bench and Amanda could have rejected Heather's invitation of friendship, but they both took a courageous step toward one another. Heather spoke simple words with profound possibilities when she offered her contact info and said, "If you want to talk or hang . . ." The scene ends with the encouraging picture of Amanda no longer alone but seated on the bench beside Heather.

Flourish in Helping Others During Deployment

Family separations are inherent to military life. Deployment, training, and various schools for the military service member will all happen—and happen again. A commitment to seek community is key and essential to making it through a military family separation. In the movie, Heather reached out to Amanda, and they found in each other a battle buddy. Their shared military experience provided an immediate bond that became a support system throughout the deployment. They both understood the challenge of war for the family member at home. The steps they took are steps you and I can follow to help someone flourish during a deployment.

How to Flourish in Helping

1. **A step toward.** Take a courageous step toward a wife experiencing deployment. Start a conversation and find ways to offer practical help without being invasive. Simple deeds such as providing a meal, sending a note or text, making a phone call, and if she's a mom—offering to watch her children, can be the thing that turns the tide of a day during a deployment.

2. **A step beside**. Come alongside and offer a safe space to express emotions. Guard against telling a deployed wife to just "be positive," but help her not get stuck in the negative.

3. **A step ahead**. Continue to reach out to offer words of encouragement and acts of service throughout the deployment. Think ahead and find out about birthdays, anniversaries, or other significant days where you could provide support.

Flourish in Helping Others During Deployment

Verses to Consider

Therefore encourage one another and build each other up, just as you are doing (1 Thess. 5:11).

But exhort one another every day, as long as it is called "today," that none of you may be hardened by the deceitfulness of sin (Heb. 3:13).

And let us consider how to stir up one another to love and good works, not neglecting to meet together, as is the habit of some, but encouraging one another, and all the more as you see the Day drawing near (Heb. 10:24–25).

Prayer

Lord, strengthen the sister who is alone today because of a military deployment or separation. Encourage her through the power of your Holy Spirit and intersect her life with someone who will sit with her, walk with her, talk with her, and be a friend who shares your love. Amen.

14

Flourish in Homecoming

By Liz Giertz

Military families constantly face troubling transitions from relocation to reenlistment to retirement. Perhaps the hardest and most likely to fail is the reintegration of the uniformed military member back into family life following a deployment.

The whole world weeps tears of joy with us as they watch welcome home ceremonies. While we do enjoy big and small benefits with reunification (ahem . . . an end to forced celibacy), one of the greatest myths about military life is that everything is rainbows and unicorns when the military member returns home. Quite honestly, military families are guilty of encouraging the spread of this falsehood.

We pretend everything is wonderful because that is what the world expects of us. Since we recognize that there are many who are less fortunate, we constantly say how grateful we are to be under the same roof again. We use the excuse of exhaustion and the need for quality family time to make up for our lack of social engagement because it sounds better than admitting we're struggling to find our groove as a family again. But what if we got honest and admitted our struggles to ourselves and each other? When I am brave enough to admit the mess, I discover I'm not alone.

Just like a wedding is only the beginning of a marriage, the welcome home ceremony is only the tip of the iceberg of reintegration. We become like newlyweds, learning to live together again, only we bring more baggage to the party this time around. Husbands have changed. Wives have changed. Children have changed. It doesn't matter if the deployment was ninety days or fifteen months, the time apart changes us all.

While the streets of Baghdad are more stressful for the service member than a desk job in Kuwait, simply having the service member absent produces anxiety in the spouse and children who wait at home. After returning home, difficult discussions we didn't have time for during the deployment are doubly hard. Unmet expectations still sting. Neither party really knows the full extent of what went on while they were apart. The one who was away is often stinky and starving after traveling for days on end, and the one who was home is frayed and frazzled after making grand preparations for the big day. Both are exhausted. As good as it is to be in each other's arms again, there is a grieving for the closeness of the support network they knew during the deployment.

If you have endured a deployment of any length this probably sounds familiar. Even though it doesn't sound like a formula for flourishing to me, there is help and hope. Here are five tactics I have discovered to flourish in homecomings.

How to Flourish in Homecomings

1. **Communicate effectively.** It's easy to blame unmet expectations for our problems in marriage, but the root cause is usually a failure to communicate. Expectations we don't communicate are just wishes. No matter how much we might think our spouses should, no one can read minds. If we haven't communicated and been understood, we lose our right to feel hurt. Use the time after a deployment to rediscover your spouse's best method for communication.

2. **Be intentional.** Do something together. One way to close the distance between you and your spouse is for you both to grow closer to God. A couples' Bible study would be a great way to remember why you fell in love in the first place. It can help you reconnect and reopen the lines of communication.

3. **Set goals.** The natural pause created by the end of a deployment enables us to make changes that might otherwise feel awkward. We can assess our lives and

families and make plans to improve in the short and the long term. Setting goals as a couple encourages us to have a shared vision for our family and gives us something to work toward together.

4. **Be honest.** Commit to transparency with yourself, your spouse, and those in your inner circle of support. Don't be afraid to ask them to pray in specific ways about your transition. Even hiding hard truths with good intentions can cause a divide when discovered.

5. **Get help.** Many agencies are available to help military families navigate transitions. Getting help for your marriage and your family doesn't make you weak, it makes you a fighter! God created and placed each of us strategically in community because he intends for us to help one another.

And here's a truth you can stand on during the challenge of homecomings:

No matter how much things seem to have changed, God never does. We can rely on him to remain faithful, loving, and always working for our best interest. When we believe this and trust him, we can flourish no matter how tough the transition feels.

Verses to Consider

And we know that for those who love God all things work together for good, for those who are called according to his purpose (Rom. 8:28).

A soft answer turns away wrath, but a harsh word stirs up anger (Prov. 15:1).

Bear one another's burdens, and so fulfill the law of Christ (Gal. 6:2).

Prayer

Lord, as we approach the end of a deployment, prepare our hearts for this transition. May we grow closer to you and each other, and not apart. Bring the help we need to truly flourish. Amen.

15

Flourish in Connecting

By Kori Yates

Our oldest was less than a year old the first time we walked through a deployment with children. Our daughter had no idea who my husband was when he came home after a year-long deployment. The next few weeks brought strange looks as she wondered why this random person showed up in our house. Each day she had tactile curiosity as she felt his hairy arms (a strange feeling when you've been around women your whole life). Adjusting to the deep voice brought crocodile tears . . .from daddy and daughter. Reintegration was interesting but being able to help a child readjust after a deployment was more about me than her.

As we added each child and as they grew, future deployments were a bit different. The older they got the more they recognized the separation, missed their daddy, wrestled with the "what if," and asked a million questions about what he was doing and when he would be home. I was determined that all of us, my husband included, would thrive during this time—and thrive we did.

Helping children understand and adjust to a deployment challenges the best of parents. In Acts 20:24, Paul is walking into something he knows will be challenging. In fact, Paul is certain he will never again see those to whom he is writing. His perspective, though, is one we have focused on in our family, even during times of separation. Paul's desire was to fulfill his calling to "testify to the gospel of the grace of God." Shouldn't this be our desire too? Shouldn't we teach this same thing to our children? Our lives are woven intentionally by a loving God. He has a purpose and plan, even for deployments.

As we have walked with our children through deployments, we continue to point them to Jesus. We seek out the things God has done and the blessings he has given. We remember that our mission as a family remains the same, even if we're geographically separated. Regardless of location, we are still a family.

In these seasons God has truly blessed us. However, it is not all flowers and rainbows. We have days that are challenging and hard. Anxiety knocks at the doors of our hearts and threatens to take over. We have moments when we are lonely and sad. However, even though we wrestle with these things, we (and our children) can still stay connected during the separations of military life.

Our children were older during our last deployment, so I took this opportunity to ask them what things we had done during deployments that helped us thrive. The list they shared with me is what I am sharing with you. Some of the things I thought were important during a deployment weren't even blips on my children's radar. Children are all different. Ask yours.

How to Flourish in Connecting

1. **Have fun with communication.** My kids loved to video chat and send messages during deployments. Some of their favorite things were sending emojis or gifs. It was super funny when they sent the puking emoji. When they get something back it becomes hysterical. They also enjoyed sending goofy pictures of themselves or random shots of our activities. At the end of their day though, that snail-mail letter sure hit the spot.

2. **Send some love.** My kids apparently LOVE to send care packages. We've put together themed ones and random ones. It was even more fun when it was opened on the other end. This was their favorite way to connect during a deployment.

3. **Take time to dream.** My children also enjoyed dreaming about what we would do together when deployment was over. Those discussions didn't include huge vacations. They focused more on time together, like sharing favorite meals, watching movies, playing

catch, simply enjoying everyday activities. We had many of these chats, both in our home and via Skype.

4. **Do life.** They liked that we still did life when Dad was gone. We still had friends over, went to the pool, went on a road trip, hung out with the neighbors, and attended church. Life didn't screech to a halt. However, we did curtail some of our activities since there was only one parent at home, but they have good memories even during deployment.

5. **Take time with Jesus.** This one is my contribution. I found it of utmost importance for both the parents and the children to spend time reading God's word, talking about it, and praying together. It doesn't have to be every day for a certain period of time but connecting with Christ and letting His word encourage and strengthen us is truly the key to flourishing.

Verses to Consider

But I do not account my life of any value nor as precious to myself, if only I may finish my course and the ministry that I received from the Lord Jesus, to testify to the gospel of the grace of God (Acts 20:24).

For this reason I bow my knees before the Father, from whom every family in heaven and on earth is named, that according to the riches of his glory he may grant you to be strengthened with power through his Spirit in your inner being, so that Christ may dwell in your hearts through faith—that you, being rooted and grounded in love, may have strength to comprehend with all the saints what is the breadth and length and height and depth, and to know the love of Christ that surpasses knowledge, that you may be filled with all the fullness of God (Eph. 3:14–19).

Count it all joy, my brothers, when you meet trials of various kinds, for you know that the testing of your faith produces steadfastness (James 1:2–3).

Prayer

Lord, teach my children to see you even during a deployment. Through your grace and love, I pray that we will not simply survive this season, but truly flourish. Only through you, Lord. Amen.

16

Flourish in Agreement

By Liz Giertz

When our oldest son was born, I labored through the night with my mom by my side, unable to reach my husband in Iraq. By the grace of God, someone found him while he was checking guard towers, whisking him to the phone just before my contractions made it impossible for me to talk anymore. He met his firstborn son in person nearly twelve weeks later, but he was only able spend a fourteen-day "honeymoon" period with us before returning to Iraq. I spent most of the next five months raising and training our son alone. My main goal was to teach him to sleep in his own crib.

We established a routine that allowed me to get him up, dressed, fed, and my son to daycare in time for me to fall in for PT formation. In the evenings, we did our own thing. He had all my attention from the time I picked him up from daycare until his eyes closed at night. I had bedtime down to a science. I bathed him, read him a book, said prayers while nursing, and plopped him down on his back in the crib before his eyes fully closed, giving him the chance to self-soothe.

After the Welcome Home ceremony upon my soldier's return, imagine my chagrin when I found my husband singing and rocking our child to sleep in his arms those first few nights. Truth be told, at first, I thought it was incredibly sweet to watch my handsome, tough soldier snuggle our infant. I realized our son was losing the ability to fall asleep on his own, risking all my hard work and discipline.

Most early childhood experts agree that when it comes to the discipline and training of children, success is more likely to be achieved when the parents agree on their methodology. Parenting is hard enough (like running a daily marathon tough) when both parents live under the same roof. But parenting on the same page is even harder when you are separated for extended periods of time.

Eventually I took off my own military uniform, we added a second son to the mix, and my husband deployed and traveled for work several more times. I learned reestablishing parenting routines only gets more challenging as our children grow older. Late nights, frequent training exercises, temporary duty, and deployments make it hard for military families to parent in agreement.

However, God has taught us that his page is the most important one to be on for parenting. When we intentionally adhere to God's principles for parenting, we pass on eternally important values to our children, no matter how many deployments, TDYs, or field training exercises. Believe it or not, none of them require us to reside under the same roof.

How to Flourish in Agreement

1. **Communicate.** Effective communication is the bedrock of parenting in agreement. If we aren't sharing plans and processes with our parenting partners, we have no expectation that we will share a common vision or execution of that vision. Without communication, everything else crumbles. Children do not flourish with mixed messages. Parents must be clear and concise in communicating expectations and consequences, both with each other and with their children.

2. **Balance Law and grace.** I used to joke that in our parenting arrangements I was the Law and my husband was the Gospel. Some days that does flip flop. One thing we've noticed is the need to appropriately balance the two if we expect to maintain healthy discipline in our home without crushing the spirits of our children. This is how God parents his children. He uses the Law to point out our faults, but he doesn't leave us to wallow in our messes. He sent Jesus to die on the cross to give us eternal hope. The Holy Spirit

leads us in the way we should go. As parents, we must also embrace this balanced approach.

3. **Point to God as father.** As a mother, I found great comfort in the realization that God is a perfect parent, even though his kids are often unruly and disobedient, myself included. My children have seen me mess up more than most people. By turning to God for forgiveness, we can quit trying to pretend we're perfect. Instead, we can look to Jesus who was flawless for us. Always pointing to God is the way we parent on the same page, and how we impart what is eternally important.

Verses to Consider

And these words that I command you today shall be on your heart. You shall teach them diligently to your children, and shall talk of them when you sit in your house, and when you walk by the way, and when you lie down, and when you rise (Deut. 6:6–7).

All Scripture is breathed out by God and profitable for teaching, for reproof, for correction, and for training in righteousness, that the man of God may be complete, equipped for every good work (2 Tim. 3:16–17).

Children, obey your parents in everything, for this pleases the Lord. Fathers, do not provoke your children, lest they become discouraged (Col. 3:20–21).

Prayer

Lord, thank you for the example you set for parenting. I depend on you for wisdom each day. Help me to impart what's eternally important to my children. Amen.

17

Flourish in Teenage Years

By Muriel Gregory

Ten years ago, I was not looking forward to parenting a teenager. Watching movies and hearing horror stories from other parents made me terrified of teen angst, hormones, and rebellion. In comparison, potty training seemed like a breeze.

When my daughter turned thirteen, I officially became the mom of a teenager. A well-meaning friend had warned me that our relationship would change and my daughter would become distant. The thought saddened me, but I braced myself for it. Eighteen months later, my son became a teenager as well. A chapter had closed. Nothing but teenage children in the home.

So, I prayed. A lot. I prayed for God to give me wisdom to keep a good balance. How would I let them spread their wings, but still be their mom? How would I help them be successful as they moved toward more autonomy? Their budding independence prompted me to rethink my parenting. My disciplining morphed into discipling. They were still my children, however, I also began to see them as disciples.

Mistakes were made by all. Poor choices made by my children led to hurts and disappointments. It was hard to watch my children make mistakes.

When a caterpillar transforms into a butterfly it struggles tremendously. However, if we help the butterfly emerge from the cocoon, we sentence it to death. The butterfly needs the struggle to strengthen its wings, enabling it to fly free in the world. The same is true with our teenagers. Watching them flail can tempt us to remove the hurt and to solve their problems. This labor of love is necessary for them to grow into beautiful butterflies.

How to Flourish in the Teenage Years

1. **Be present and engage them.** Teenagers, more than anything else, need our engagement. Stay *truly* connected in a digitally over-connected world. Use every opportunity to talk and listen. Allow them to vent their emotions without judgment. When they start talking, take notice, and ask them to tell you more.

2. **Meet them where they are.** One way to create an environment best suited for communication is to meet them where they are. What does your teenager like to do? What makes them feel safe and loved. My daughter and I would have tea together. One son loved video games. So, I would sit with him in his room, and we would talk about the game he was playing. My other son loves board games. Some of our best conversations happened at the game table.

3. **Engage around the dinner table.** Sit down as a family. Talk about the day and share life. Listen to them with your ears and your heart. Teenagers need a safe place.

Military children, more than other children, struggle with identity. *Where am I from? Who are my friends? How will I fit in at this new school? Will I make the soccer team?* Conversation at the dinner table allows them to talk about those fears. The safe place you create, the love you give, and the genuine way you engage are the foundation for a sound identity.

4. **Give them your trust.** Your teens will make mistakes, and they will hurt you, yet they need to know you trust them. Confusion is an unavoidable part of teenage years. Uncertain about themselves and the world around them, chaos often rules their minds. Be their anchor and trust them.

5. **Pray diligently.** Let your children know you pray for them. Pray that the Word of God you speak over them will not return void (Isaiah 55:11). Ask God to finish the good work he started in them (Philippians 1:6). Pray that God will shepherd them as he shepherds us (Psalm 23:1).

6. **Encourage your teen's faith.** Talk about the faithfulness of God. Tell them God knows what they need (Matthew 6:32). Reassure them of how much

God cares for them (1 Peter 5:7). Encourage them to seek God for answers (Luke 11:9–13).

I have made plenty of mistakes as a parent. The greatest lesson I learned is that even though my children were growing up, that did not mean we were growing apart. Parenting teens may look different year to year, but I will always be their mom. God gives us the tools, guidance, and wisdom we need to flourish in the teenage years.

Verses to Consider

So shall my word be that goes out from my mouth; it shall not return to me empty, but it shall accomplish that which I purpose, and shall succeed in the thing for which I sent it (Isa. 55:11).

For everything there is a season and a time for every matter under heaven: a time to be born, and a time to die; a time to plant, and a time to pluck up what is planted; . . . (Ecc. 3:1–2).

Train up a child in the way he should go; even when he is old he will not depart from it (Prov. 22:6).

Prayer

Lord, thank you for the perfect example you have set for us. Thank you for granting wisdom I need as I grow up with our children. Thank you for the gift of parenting because it sharpens my faith. Amen.

18

Flourish in Parenting Adults

By Brenda Pace

"I feel like someone chopped off an appendage!" That was how I described our family's move to Washington, D.C. when my oldest son was a senior in high school. He left for college while we moved to a new place. He would come "home" during school breaks, but that new place never felt like home to him. The transition felt brusque and harsh—at least for this mama.

The adjustment in parent-child roles can feel sudden for military families when home base suddenly changes and is unfamiliar for the child who has moved out of the house. The shift in roles from being the supervisor of daily activities to that of encourager and mentor of an adult child is a necessary adjustment for parents and children. Even though it is inevitable, it can be painful.

Do you think Mary felt some of the same emotions we do, as her parenting role with Jesus shifted?

On the third day there was a wedding at Cana in Galilee, and the mother of Jesus was there. Jesus also was invited to the wedding with his disciples. When the wine ran out, the mother of Jesus said to him, "They have no wine." And Jesus said to her, "Woman, what does this have to do with me? My hour has not yet come." His mother said to the servants, "Do whatever he tells you" (John 2:1–5).

After this event in Cana, things were never the same. The response of Jesus to Mary's request may seem harsh to our Western way of thinking, but when Jesus addressed Mary as *woman*, he took the necessary step toward redefining their roles. His identity moved from son to Savior. He willingly responded to her request to do something to help the bride and groom, but he did not do it under her authority. This time he moved in the authority granted to him by God. Mary set a lovely example by her response. She did not take offense, question him, or rebuke him for his reply. She trusted him to do the right thing, illustrated by her command, "Do whatever he tells you."

How to Flourish in Parenting Adult Children

1. **Release.** The act of release and relinquishment may take courage and discipline. I realize I must release my adult children to make their own decisions and provide much encouragement and little commentary.

2. **Respect.** I must respect the boundaries my children set as they flex their adult wings. Healthy relationships require respect and room to grow. I give them a gift when I respect them as adults, especially in the way I speak to them. I want my tone, words, and actions to communicate grace and respect.

3. **Reliance.** I can trust that what my husband and I taught and instilled in our children is in their hearts and minds. The way they walk that out may look different than I imagined, but that is okay. Through intercessory prayer for my children, I place my reliance on God, knowing he loves them more than I, and he will direct them.

Verses to Consider

Hear, my son, your father's instruction, and forsake not your mother's teaching, for they are a graceful garland for your head and pendants for your neck (Prov. 1:8–9).

And stretching out his hand toward his disciples, he said, "Here are my mother and my brothers! For whoever does the will of my Father in heaven is my brother and sister and mother" (Matt. 12:49–50).

Go therefore and make disciples of all nations, baptizing them in the name of the Father and of the Son and of the Holy Spirit (Matt. 28:19).

Prayer

I regularly pray this Scripture from Ephesians 3:14–19 for my adult children—and their children:

Lord, for this reason I bow my knees before the Father, from whom every family in heaven and on earth is named, that according to the riches of his glory he may grant you to be strengthened with power through his Spirit in your inner being, so that Christ may dwell in your hearts through faith. That you, being rooted and grounded in love, may have strength to comprehend with all the saints what is the breadth and length and height and depth, and to know the love of Christ that surpasses knowledge. That you may be filled with all the fullness of God. Amen.

19

Flourish in Loss

By Claudia Duff

Izzy T was our first grandbaby. Though military life kept us far from our adult children, we loved his precious heart the moment we heard the news from my oldest son: "We are having a baby, and it's a boy!" We could not have been happier. I counted the days to his birth with more excitement than waiting for the end of a deployment. A few short months later, our hearts were crushed and held captive by unthinkable grief when he died. Grief felt thick as molasses, cold as ice, and thorny as a rose bush. There seemed to be no escape from this tremendous feeling of loss.

I lose things all the time: my keys, my purse, my coffee cup, my favorite shoes. Just about anything I am supposed to have a grip on I have lost. But do you know what? I always find these things. Always. But not this time. The loss of Izzy T was permanent.

When you suffer the loss of a child, not many want to support you outside of Facebook, cards, and emails. It's a loss most do not want to get close to. Why? Because it's scary. The possibility of loss is there for anyone, and that makes it scary. If it happened to you, it could happen to me. I don't want to talk about that or even entertain the thought. When an infant dies, feeling alone and abandoned in grief takes the shape of lost hope.

However, God is faithful, and he has promised to be with us in the "valley of the shadow of death." This is the moment when the saints must take their places in the valley with those who are "walking through." In grief, we need the love and support of family and friends.

> *When you pass through the waters, I will be with you; and through the rivers, they shall not overwhelm you; when you walk through fire you shall not be burned, and the flame shall not consume you* (Isa. 43:2).

I've read this verse more times than I care to count. I never felt the full weight of it until we lost Izzy T. I couldn't quite catch my breath, as if the waters of grief were surely going to overwhelm me. The fire of sadness seemed to burn right through my broken heart, leaving me with a feeling of being scorched alive.

Yet, God.

He brought me through the waters of loss and the flames of grief. Even on my worst days when I laid in bed crying, the Lord met me in ways I didn't know were possible. God's promises are exact, penetrating the places we hold tight. They demolish all the things that seek to destroy us. God does that through the ministry of the Holy Spirit, through his Word, and through the saints.

God plans for those who believe to stand with those who are grieving. Are you overwhelmed by grief and sorrow? If not, could you help a grieving friend or relative? God often works through people to comfort the hurting. We only need to look in the Bible to discover the strategies of a gracious God to overcome the evil schemes of the enemy. You see, the enemy desires to use our grief to kill our faith, steal our joy, and destroy our testimony. Yet, God promises to be with us, and his promises are true.

How to Flourish Even in the Loss of a Child

1. **Communicate with those who love you.** Answer your phone. Most people will find it hard to make that call. If you are not feeling up to speaking, listen to the voice mail. Why? Because our hearts need to be reminded that someone is for us, that they are praying and thinking of us. It helps our souls not feel so alone. Read the text and respond. God will continue to move on your behalf by stirring them to pray for you again and again.

2. **Reach out for specific help.** I received quite a few messages from people reaching out and sharing their personal stories. I contacted some of them individually. It was such a gift to have someone who had been through the same thing listening to me and validating my sorrow with their own.

3. **Seek professional help if needed.** See a doctor. I had a friend make me promise to see a doctor if I still wasn't getting dressed and leaving my house after ninety days. I made the call and sobbed through the

entire process of making an appointment. Do it. The professionals are there for a reason—they know more than we do and can help.

4. **Join a church small group**. There are many opportunities within churches to join in with others. This wasn't my preference, but it might be yours. Try it.

5. **Cry when you need to.** I cried every day. However, the most significant day of crying happened when a friend drove five hours to sit in my living room and let me cry on her shoulder. It was unexpected. Even now as I type, I am moved to tears. She took "weep with those who weep" to a personal level. I will forever be changed by her generosity of love.

6. **Continue to develop your faith.** Read your Bible. The Word of God saved my life every single day. God's promises held my grip to his grace. It grounded me when I felt lost in my sorrow. Go to church. I wanted to hide away because I didn't want to see happy people or listen to them say, "Sorry for your loss." However, sometimes what we don't want is what we need. Being surrounded by "such a great cloud of witnesses" is a good thing. Journal. One day you will be the saint

called to sit, listen, and pray for someone else who is where you are now. It will be a tremendous gift to have written words that affirm what you know to be true.

Izzy T is our grandson. As grandparents, our loss was not quite the same as that felt by our son and sweet daughter-in-love. Consequently, I was determined not to allow my loss to overshadow theirs. It takes commitment to pray for them more than I pray for myself. Watching my firstborn son say goodbye to his first-born son took my breath away. Watching him comfort his wife as they held their son for the first and last time was not something I want to remember

But, God.

Listening to my son say, "WE will get through this. God will help us," was transforming. Watching them cling to one another as they both held fast to faith was awe-inspiring. These two young people loving one another and walking by faith only a few months into their second year of marriage humbled me. I learned from them what it means to believe without seeing anything new happen. Infant loss is not something we prepare for, but God does. He is right where we are. Be encouraged because God will fight for you, you need only to believe.

Verses to Consider

And I said to the nobles and to the officials and to the rest of the people, "The work is great and widely spread, and we are separated on the wall, far from one another. In the place where you hear the sound of the trumpet, rally to us there. Our God will fight for us" (Neh. 4:19–20).

Be gracious to me, O Lord, for I am in distress; my eye is wasted from grief; my soul and my body also (Psa. 31:9).

He was despised and rejected by men, a man of sorrows and acquainted with grief; and as one from whom men hide their faces he was despised, and we esteemed him not (Isa. 53:3).

Prayer

Lord, in this place of profound loss, meet me. When my heart becomes overwhelmed by the hopelessness of death, overtake me by your grace. Make my brokenness bow to your new mercies every morning. Rally saints to walk alongside me through prayer and words of comfort. Help me to seek you above all else and bring about your glory in this loss. Amen.

20

Flourish in Prayer

By Ginger Harrington

When my husband deployed to the Middle East, I prayed for his safety daily. "Lord, please watch over my husband and keep him safe." During each of our moves, I prayed my way through the months of settling into new places. "Lord, please bless my children in this new place. Help us to make good friends and get used to a new community." When problem solving and making decisions today, I ask for God's guidance. "Lord, show me how to solve my problem. Please guide me in this decision."

Praying about our needs and concerns allows us to flourish in our spiritual life. Over the years God has changed the way I pray. I used to approach prayer as seeking answers to questions or provision for needs. It was an exchange—my prayers for God's answers. Now I understand that prayer is not a formula, nor is it a transaction or bargaining tool for getting God to do what we want.

Prayer is a vital part of our intimacy and relationship with God, a way to communicate and be present. Too often I prayed to "get something" I wanted or needed. To be honest, that is still a frequent mindset in my prayers. As we mature in faith, our prayer needs to include both asking for God's help and seeking to know his heart. To flourish in prayer, we need to reach beyond request-driven prayer as we deepen our relationship with God.

Living in communion with God we learn that prayer is the way we enjoy God and he enjoys us. Practically speaking, we seek God when we pray. Psalm 73 inspires me to desire him more:

> *Nevertheless I am continually with you . . . there is nothing on earth that I desire besides you. My flesh and my heart may fail, but God is the strength of my heart and my portion forever . . . But for me it is good to be near God; I have made the Lord GOD my refuge . . .* (Psa. 73: 23–26, 28).

Sometimes prayer is trusting that God knows what we are experiencing. He knows our hurts, understands our struggles, and loves us during it all. Because he invites us to pray, we can let go of the pressure to pray "pretty prayers" that sound good. Flourishing in prayer is living in an authentic connection with God, trusting that he listens to us. Be honest and real with God. Pour out your heart as you abide in him and trust in his Word. He already knows all the details, but prayer reminds us to rely on him and not on ourselves.

God knows our hearts and is well acquainted with our needs. He even knows what we're going to say before the words form in our mouths. "You search out my path and my lying down and are acquainted with all my ways. Even before a word is on my tongue, behold, O LORD, you know it altogether" (Psa. 139:3–4).

Simple prayers often best convey our true thoughts and needs in the moment.

"Help me, Lord,"

"I trust you, Father."

"You know what I need."

"I love you, Lord."

"Help me to pray."

"What do you want me to learn in this situation?"

Prayer connects our hearts with God's. When we believe God is good, faithful, and present, we begin to trust him even when we struggle to understand our circumstances.

How to Flourish in Prayer

1. **Pray in the moment.** Keep a continuous conversation with God. Talk with him throughout the day (Ephesians 6:18, 1 Thessalonians 5:17).

2. **Pray with confidence, trusting in God's grace and mercy.** God has invited you to pray, to come confidently whenever you have a need for mercy, help, or grace. Military life often requires strength beyond our reserves. Take him at his word by praying with the assurance that he welcomes your prayer (Hebrews 4:16, Hebrews 10: 19–22).

3. **Pray with a thankful heart.** Gratitude changes our perspective, shifting our attention from our problem to God's power and presence (Philippians 4:6–7, Psalm 100:4, Colossians 4:2).

4. **Ask God to help you pray when you're not sure what or how to pray.** The Holy Spirit helps us to pray in a variety of ways. Prayers don't always have right words and we don't always know what to ask for. Trust the Spirit to help you pray (Romans 8:26).

5. **Watch to see what God does next.** Pray with anticipation that God will work through your prayer. Let go of the expectation of a certain answer as you trust that God will respond. Surrender your desires by trusting that God will give the best answer (Psalm 5:3, Habakkuk 2:1–3, Colossians 4:2).

Verses to Consider

Let us then with confidence draw near to the throne of grace, that we may receive mercy and find grace to help in time of need (Heb. 4:16).

Likewise the Spirit helps us in our weakness. For we do not know what to pray for as we ought, but the Spirit himself intercedes for us with groanings too deep for words (Rom. 8:26).

Continue steadfastly in prayer, being watchful in it with thanksgiving (Col. 4:2).

Prayer

Lord, thank you for the gift of prayer. Continue to teach me to pray as I seek a deeper relationship with you. I want to know you more fully as I share my life with you in prayer. Amen.

21

Flourish in Praying Like Jesus

By Brenda Pace

Some mornings I feel like if getting up early was an object, I would break it, burn it, and bury it where it could never be found again. I read these words on a greeting card and nodded. Anyone associated with the military knows about getting up at "0' dark thirty." If you have lived on a military installation you may have been awakened by reveille at sunrise or the singing of Jody calls during morning PT. For the night owl, this can be the personification of a rude awakening. Scripture indicates Jesus would have fit right into the morning routine of a military installation:

> *And rising very early in the morning, while it was still dark, he departed and went out to a desolate place, and there he prayed* (Mark 1:35).

Jesus quietly rose before anyone else, even though his itinerary had been intense with more pressure on the horizon. In the early morning hours, he slipped away and found a place to be alone to pray. I'm drawn to this passage in Mark 1:35 because it shows the priority of prayer of our Savior. Prayer was a part of his lifestyle. He not only prayed in the early morning, but Luke 6:12 documents him praying all night. The point is not the time, place, or length of prayer, but that we pray. The message brought out through the life and words of Jesus is that we "ought always to pray and not lose heart" (Luke 18:1).

Have you ever wondered why one of the disciples asked Jesus, "Lord, teach us to pray . . . " (Luke 11:1)? He did not ask for lessons on preaching, healing, evangelizing, or casting out demons, but "teach us to pray." Could it be this disciple made the connection between the power of Jesus and his prayer life?

While the Lord's Prayer is a model for his followers, Jesus showed by example that prayer is the number one way to flourish in our relationship with God. A simple definition of prayer is communication with God—and good communication is the foundational element of any relationship. Jesus demonstrated a pattern of good communication with the Father through his life of prayer.

In addition to Jesus' example and teaching on prayer, I've often been encouraged by this prayer from E. Stanley Jones:

"Gracious Christ, teach me to pray. For if I fall down here, I fall down everywhere—anemia spreads through my whole being. Give me the mind to pray, the love to pray, the will to pray. Let prayer be the aroma of every act, the atmosphere of every thought, my native air. In Your name. Amen."[4]

---

4 E Stanley Jones, *How to Pray* (Nashville:Upper Room Books, 2015), 45.

How to Flourish in Praying Like Jesus

1. **Pray for others.** *. . . but I have prayed for you, that your faith may not fail* (Luke 22:32).

2. **Pray regularly.** *And he came out and went, as was his custom, to the Mount of Olives, and the disciples followed him* (Luke 22:39).

3. **Pray before decisions.** *In these days he went out to the mountain to pray, and all night he continued in prayer to God. And when day came, he called his disciples and chose from them twelve, whom he named apostles* (Luke 6:12–13).

4. **Pray for God's will.** *. . . saying, "Father, if you are willing, remove this cup from me. Nevertheless, not my will, but yours, be done"* (Luke 22:42).

5. **Pray in confidence that God hears you.** *And Jesus lifted up his eyes and said, "Father, I thank you that you have heard me"* (John 11:41b).

6. **Pray alone.** *But he would withdraw to desolate places and pray* (Luke 5:16).

7. **Pray with others.** *Now about eight days after these sayings he took with him Peter and John and James and went up on the mountain to pray* (Luke 9:28).

These ways to pray are not complicated or costly, but they are powerful and valuable. Learning to pray like Jesus is the key to flourishing in our relationship with God. Which step will you take today?

Verses to Consider

In the days of his flesh, Jesus offered up prayers and supplications, with loud cries and tears, to him who was able to save him from death, and he was heard because of his reverence (Heb. 5:7).

Who is to condemn? Christ Jesus is the one who died—more than that, who was raised—who is at the right hand of God, who indeed is interceding for us (Rom. 8:34).

And whatever you ask in prayer, you will receive, if you have faith (Matt. 21:22).

Prayer

Lord, thank you that you listen and are attentive to my prayers. I pray with the disciples, "Teach me to pray." May prayer be my first words in the morning and my last words at night. Open my ears to hear your voice as I depend on you for wisdom and guidance throughout each day. Amen.

22

Flourish in Intentional Prayer

By Claudia Duff

I can't remember a time in my life when I didn't pray. Even as a child, I whispered many prayers to Jesus. Not because I was so holy from the start, but because I was so incredibly desperate. A Sunday school teacher told me about God who loved me, promised to never leave me, never hurt me, and one day he would come and take me to live with him forever. I have never looked back, only forward. Prayer has been my linchpin, my tether to the heart of God.

This life often takes my breath away in both good and bad ways. Watching my children grow into mature believers has been the best. Watching them slip and fall in their faith, not so much. The things challenges of this world will often take us to our knees, and at times to our faces.

A few years ago, the Lord impressed upon me the need to pray more intentionally. Even though I have always prayed, my prayer has not always been as deliberate as it is now. God is teaching me how to, "Rejoice in hope, be patient in tribulation, be constant in prayer" (Romans 12:12). My prayer life cannot exist on a whim. I must come at it with more direction.

> *Watch and pray that you may not enter into temptation. The spirit indeed is willing, but the flesh is weak* (Matt. 26:41).

Reading this verse turns my thoughts to those closest to me. This is where my prayer journey began to change. The Word of God says to watch and pray, and those who are present in my everyday life are there for the watching and the praying.

We live in a world that surrounds us daily with things that pull us away from the presence of God. What if somewhere, someone was always praying? How would that begin to shift the atmosphere in our own lives and in the lives of our loved ones? The Word of God assures us things would indeed begin to change.

I discovered that keeping a journal of my thoughts, prayers, concerns, and victories is critical for me to stay on course with my soul-care. Connecting with God is eternally important.

How to Flourish in Intentional Prayer

1. **Be patient.** When I am unsure of what to pray, I sit before the Lord silently and wait for him to speak and direct my prayers. I have been struggling with how to pray for someone very dear to me. God has been faithful to help me pray for them. Prayer is a time of listening and speaking. God listens when we speak, and we must be patient to hear when he speaks back to us. Take the time to listen.

2. **Ask for help.** Not shy when the need is deep, I don't hesitate to ask others to pray for me. I speak all the words needed to give my prayer warriors a full understanding of the gravity of my need. The Lord has faithfully granted me people who speak mighty truths into my heart. I treasure them and have come to depend on them.

3. **Pray God's Word.** I pray the Word of God that specifically targets my prayer need. I do a word search in one of my Bible apps for my prayer need. This year my word is "peace." I search for verses about peace, copy them in my journal, and pray them for myself.

4. **Write the prayers.** I write the prayers in my journal. When I read past journals I see such growth in my faith. I can see in my own written words how God has delivered me from the deepest places of sorrows when I wondered if I would survive. However, God did it, and I have written proof. (Of course, if you are my close friend, and you all are, you know to burn ALL those leather journals when I die. And I am not even kidding!)

5. **Set an alarm.** I set aside times for daily prayer. I have a daily quiet time in the morning, but I do most of my praying with my prayer alarms. I have three set each day, although I will add short-term alarms for specific requests. Prayer alarms make me stop and pray intentionally, if only for a moment. I am thinking of those specific people and truly whispering a prayer on their behalf.

Learning to pray intentionally has changed me. When my heart settles into the truth of God's Word, my thoughts, fears, or circumstances do not overwhelm me. Pray intentionally today.

Verses to Consider

He brought me out into a broad place; he rescued me, because he delighted in me (Psa. 18:19).

O God, hear my prayer; give ear to the words of my mouth (Psa. 54:2).

You also must help us by prayer, so that many will give thanks on our behalf for the blessing granted us through the prayers of many (2 Cor. 1:11).

Prayer

Lord, make my heart to bow readily to the prompting of the Holy Spirit in prayer. Move me to pray intentionally. Help me to pray with focus and faith. Amen.

23

Flourish in Ceaseless Prayer

By Muriel Gregory

Pray without ceasing. I remember the challenge when I first read 1 Thessalonians 5:17. I also recall the frustration of not knowing how to pray all the time. How was I supposed to do that when a million other things were begging for my attention?

I am grateful for the wise teachers and mentors who have crossed my path through the years, shedding light on my questions. Bible studies and prayer groups have sharpened my understanding of prayer. Life's unknowns, however, have provided the prompter for a majority of my "on the spot prayers."

New orders . . . pray.

Promotion list . . . pray.

Parenting . . . pray.

Teenager driving . . . pray and pray some more.

Deployment . . . pray.

In each situation, I poured out my fears, anxieties, worries, and requests to God. Then, mercifully, peace swaddled my heart like a cozy blanket.

Along the way, I learned that praying also meant thanking God for the many blessings in my life. A small acknowledgment of the provisions God poured into my daily activities was reasonable.

Door to door PCS (yes, they do happen) . . . praise.

Potty training success . . . praise.

Great neighbors at the new duty station . . . praise.

A wedding anniversary and he is home with me . . . praise.

A friend's sweet note in dark times . . . praise.

One of the things I love the most about God is his relentless pursuit of my heart. He longs to be with us, and prayer is the portal to deeper intimacy with him.

After many years of practicing going deeper in prayer, I have found a secret of praying without ceasing. Let's call it prayer circles. I want you to picture Russian Nesting Dolls. To get to the smallest doll, you need to open the big one first. Let's do that.

The biggest doll (aka the outer prayer circle) is the prayer you whisper to acknowledge God's presence right here, right now. It is the listening prayer. Stay there a while and breathe deeply. God is omnipresent—he is with us everywhere, all the time. Yet, I can fill a whole day with chores, activities, friends, and family, and forget to recognize his presence with me.

The second doll is the missional prayer to a mission-focused God. As adopted children in his family we have the privilege of joining him on his mission to share his love and care with others. As God the Father sent his son Jesus, so Jesus sends us into the world empowered by the Holy Spirit. Like a good soldier, we need to pay attention to the marching orders from our Commander.

This prayer comes right after acknowledging his presence. It looks something like this: "God, I know you are in this place. I realize you are at work here. How can I join you?" When a person comes to mind, I make a point to reach out to them.

At my favorite coffee shop, God will nudge me toward a person. Nothing complicated. Sometimes a smile. At other times, small talk. I am an introvert, so at first it felt awkward. Practice helps me feel more comfortable in following God's lead. Praying missionally makes his presence real in my life, making me feel useful and more aware of my purpose. My favorite part of the day has become my missional time in prayer.

The last doll is the personal request doll. To be honest, this is the prayer I was most familiar with when I started praying this way. Still, today it is the prayer I say most often. Praying for friends, church members, family, etc., has become a routine part of my quiet time in the morning. "Give us this day our daily bread" is about our daily needs. God hears and answers. If I am not careful though, my prayer life resembles a chatterbox. I am blabbering and sending requests, but never listening or enjoying his presence. This is how I protect myself.

How to Flourish in Ceaseless Prayer

1. **Start with the listening prayer.** *Our Father in Heaven, hallowed be your name* (Matthew 6:9).

2. **Then practice the missional prayer.** *Your kingdom come, your will be done, on earth as it is in Heaven* (Matthew 6:10).

3. **Finish with the practical prayer.** *Give us this day our daily bread, and forgive us our debts, as we also have forgiven our debtors. And lead us not into temptation, but deliver us from evil* (Matthew 6:11–13).

Prayer is practicing the kingdom within. When we pray and acknowledge God, we are communing with Him and the Spirit within us. Our prayers, when fueled by the Holy Spirit, can move mountains and allow us to flourish.

Verses to Consider

Come close to God, and God will come close to you (James 4:8a NLT).

May your Kingdom come soon. May your will be done on earth, as it is in heaven (Matthew 6:10 NLT).

Pray without ceasing, give thanks in all circumstances; for this is the will of God in Christ Jesus for you (1 Thessalonians 5:17–18).

Prayer

Lord, draw close to me as I draw near to you. Make your presence tangible as I practice praying without ceasing. Thank you for the gift of the Holy Spirit who guides me into deeper intimacy with you. Amen.

24

Flourish in Money Matters

By Ellie Kay

Would you like to make smarter decisions when it comes to money matters?

When I was a young military bride, I was overwhelmed by learning to manage a household. I couldn't even consider money management since I didn't even know how to cook. I remember asking my mother how to boil an egg. She replied tongue-in-cheek, "Boil it until it floats." I had no idea she was joking, so I boiled the eggs for an hour until the water evaporated and the eggs exploded. By the way, they never floated.

Today, I have millennial daughters and military daughters-in-law who are learning to manage their own homes. I developed a guideline that can help them a little more proactively than my mother's advice helped me.

How to Flourish in Money Matters

1. **Avoid emotional spending.** Never shop online or in the store when you are depressed, sad, or lonely because you are far more likely to engage in "shopping therapy," and you will usually overspend. Be especially mindful of your emotions during deployments.

2. **Show love through actions and not things**. If you have a love language of gift-giving or if you tend to show love to others by what you buy for them, you may want to shift your point of view and save your money. Perform "acts of kindness" to show people that you love them, rather than spending money that you may not have. Military spouses may be tempted to overspend on gift-giving when the military member is called away on duty.

3. **Volunteer often**. Those people who have balance in their financial lives understand how blessed they are as they give back to their communities. To get ideas about how to help, go to your local Family Support

Center or look for an online non-profit organization that needs your skills.

4. **Err on the side of generosity.** By following the principle of giving God at least 10-percent of your income, you invite God's blessing upon your money matters (Malachi 3:10).

5. **Ask yourself is this a need or a want?** Most military families do not have unlimited financial resources, and for every purchase we make it is wise to ask ourselves this question before we buy.

6. **Play the waiting game.** Wait twenty-four hours to purchase an item to avoid impulse buying. For small- and big-ticket items, this helps you get beyond the impulse to see if it's something you truly need.

7. **Have a money buddy.** Accountability is a wonderful thing. Every woman should have a person who will ask them hard questions about sticking to a budget, paying down consumer debt, or building up a savings account. In community, you are far more likely to keep your financial commitments and become a good steward of the resources God has given.

8. **Become a master saver.** Try not to pay full price when you can get a discount. Read money savings blogs, download apps for coupon codes, and be prepared to compare prices on goods and services.

9. **Become comfortable with negotiation.** Whether you are negotiating the price of a car or bidding on an item in a yard sale, you must feel it's the best deal for you. Tell the other person, "I don't feel comfortable with that price," and be quiet. I have found that nine times out of ten, I'll get a counteroffer that is something I can live with. If I don't, I feel the freedom to walk away.

10. **Pray about money matters.** Research indicates the majority of Americans admit to praying weekly or even daily. Even a financial expert like myself needs to pray to make wise financial decisions, that people won't be able to take financial advantage of me, and that I'll be able to find the best provision for my budget. Prayer makes a huge difference.

Apply these changes in stages rather than all at once. You can build a better financial life for your military family by making one wise choice at a time.

Verses to Consider

She considers a field and buys it: with the fruit of her hands she plants a vineyard (Proverbs 31:16).

He who loves money will not be satisfied with money, nor he who loves wealth with his income; this also is vanity (Ecclesiastes 5:10).

Keep your life free from love of money, and be content with what you have, for he has said, "I will never leave you nor forsake you" (Hebrews 13:5).

Prayer

Lord, thank you for everything you have given me. Thank you for providing for me daily. Please teach me how to manage your blessings. Amen.

25

Flourish in Saving

By Kori Yates

We were newlyweds. I was a new Marine married to a young soldier. We were rich—receiving our first paychecks in active duty life and actually having a combined income. You remember, right? My car was new, as was his truck. With housing difficult to come by in Clarksville, Tennessee, we decided to buy a house. It was his duty station, and I was still living in Virginia.

After a lovely two-day honeymoon, I headed back to Virginia. Just over a year later we had one child, two vehicles, and a house—and one income. After getting out of the Marine Corps, it took time to find another job. Pulling in the reigns of our spending and starting to work through a budget brought some serious marital counseling.

In addition to our retirement account, we saved a small amount of money. This was only by God's grace, because saving was not part of our conversation. When there were only two of us, dining out was a common occurrence. Now, looking through our budget the first month, we could not believe how much we previously spent on that area alone. We learned a lot about our spending those first few months.

God revealed our income is a gift. We needed to learn to steward our money. God's plan for our lives did not include living beyond our means, yet that's exactly what we were doing. With his help we refocused. We found that in seeking him our priorities changed. We realized that having an emergency fund and saving for retirement were more important than eating out.

Jesus said in the Sermon on the Mount, "For where your treasure is, there your heart will be also" (Matthew 6:21). Our treasure in the beginning was going to the restaurant down the street. We didn't like the picture it painted of us. In the following years we established an emergency fund, paid off debt, and started saving for the future.

It is amazing how much freedom money in the bank has given us. When my husband's grandfather passed away and we went to spend the week with my mother-in-law, we were able to afford it. The time we needed new tires on the car—more than enough existed in our bank account. In those moments, I was thankful we sought the Lord about

Flourish in Saving

the use of our resources. I've learned our treasure is truly in him and not in the "stuff" we obtain, nor the things we get to do.

Living within our means allows us to not only give to missions' work, but also to save for crazy things that might happen. Government shutdown? Surely not. Mandatory retirement? Never! Family illnesses when we are thousands of miles away? Who would have ever thought?

Saving and being prepared for these things is great but this practice also provides us with the margin to give generously. Truly, this is the goal—to save to give both of money and time. It is in the saving that we can rest in God's provision and contentment with what we have, while being free to give as our hearts long to do. The opportunities to give has blessed us tremendously as we walked with the Lord.

The Lord has taught us over the years about our "treasure." Years ago, we "invested" in eating out and buying stuff. As the Lord has changed us, we now invest in our future, and in others. We are learning to buy less, enjoy meals at home, give to others, and have a plan for "after the Army." We hope we are not so strapped to an income that we don't have the freedom to follow the Lord in any way he sees fit. I pray the same for you.

How to Flourish in Saving

1. **Budget.** To save we need to have a spending plan. Knowing where our money goes and having a plan for it all is a first step to saving followed by giving.

2. **Do it together.** If you are married, these decisions need to be a two-person endeavor. I know not all marriages are in a place where that works, but it is certainly best this way. Not married? Accountability from someone you trust, who is wise with their money, is a great investment of your time.

3. **Have a goal.** To get where you are going it helps to have an idea of where that might be. Spend some time seeking the Lord. The end goal might change as the Lord guides you, but having an initial goal is vital.

4. **Get professional help.** As my husband and I have grown in this area of both investing for the long-term and saving for the short-term, we have sought out professionals who can help us understand our options and opportunities. We use Dave Ramsey's ELP (Endorsed Local Provider) service to find financial

Flourish in Saving

advisors. However you go about finding them, take the time to make sure they are teachers at heart so you can learn to eventually manage your own money. We usually interview a few of them before choosing one.

God gives so much grace in this area and has truly blessed our efforts to honor him with our finances. No doubt he will do the same with you.

Verses to Consider

For where your treasure is, there your heart will be also (Matthew 6:21).

The plans of the diligent lead surely to abundance, but everyone who is hasty comes only to poverty (Proverbs 21:5).

Precious treasure and oil are in a wise man's dwelling, but a foolish man devours it (Proverbs 21:20).

Prayer

Lord, we desire to be good stewards of all you have given, including our finances. Help us to have wisdom, to be content, to seek you, and to plan for the future. May our diligence in this today allow us to give like never before. Amen.

26

Flourish in Teaching Children About Finances

By Jennifer Wake

ID card day is a special rite of passage in the military family. When my children turned ten, my husband took them to get their military ID cards. He loved taking them to get that card. In their eyes and in the eyes of the military, that was when they became "official."

Over the years, there were other rites of passage. When they turned fifteen, it was driver's permit day. It was my privilege to take each of my children to get their permits. Then came the hard work of teaching them to drive, and the hours and hours of practicing. When they got their first job we celebrated with dinner and filled out the necessary paperwork.

Driving was a goal of all our teenagers. This provided a unique opportunity to teach them fiscal responsibility. To drive our cars, they had to have a $1,000 in the bank, and they had to give the money to us. For our family, the $1,000 would pay our insurance deductible. If they damage our vehicle in anyway, we will use the money they gave to us to pay for the damage. We won't allow them to drive alone again until they have $1,000 more in the bank.

The requirement to have $1,000 motivated them to get jobs. They worked at pet sitting and babysitting to earn the money before they had "real" jobs. Today, my married daughter and her husband have their deductible in a "no touch" savings account because of this training. Years of practice help them control their finances today.

How to Flourish in Teaching Children about Finances

1. **Earning money for "Extra Chores."** After my children turned ten, I started paying for "extra chores." I had my children do normal, everyday chores, such as making beds and washing dishes. I also had a list of "extra chores." This list contained raking, mowing, vacuuming, etc. I would pay different amounts depending on the age of the child and length of time needed to complete the chore.

2. **Start saving.** When they had $50.00 saved in a physical "piggy bank," I opened savings accounts for them. Most banks have savings accounts with opening balances as low as five dollars.

3. **Teach about tithing.** As we started saving, we also talked about tithing. They had to bring it to church and put it in the offering plate. Later, when my daughter was in college, she decided to start giving to missionary friends. She added that on top of her tithing to the church.

4. **Train about taxes.** Explain to your kids about taxes. When they get a job, it is important to teach them about withholdings and how taxes work. Taxes are important for governments to work, but many people do not explain that to their children.

5. **Basics of budgeting.** Budgeting is controlling where you spend your money. It can be as simple or complex as you would like. The key is to control your money rather than your money (or lack of money) controlling you.

Raising children is an incredible blessing. Some days it is easy. Some days it is hard. Every day they learn something. Teaching about finances will help them be successful.

Verses to Consider

Train up a child in the way he should go; even when he is old he will not depart from it (Proverbs 22:6).

Honor the Lord with your wealth and with the first fruits of all your produce; then your barns will be filled with plenty, and your vats will be bursting with wine (Proverbs 3:9–10).

The point is this: whoever sows sparingly will also reap sparingly, and whoever sows bountifully will also reap bountifully. Each one must give as he has decided in his heart, not reluctantly or under compulsion, for God loves a cheerful giver. And God is able to make all grace abound to you, so that having all sufficiency in all things at all times, you may abound in every good work (2 Corinthians 9:6–8).

Prayer

Lord, please keep our kids safe every day. Teach them to use their earnings to bless others. Help us to teach them to use money wisely. Amen.

27

Flourish in Not Overspending

By Courtney Woodruff

My fingertips brushed the bright floral fabric. The light-hearted tangerine, lemon, and grapefruit hues lifted my spirits. Without a second thought I casually tossed the pretty summer dress into the shopping cart. Grinning at my baby boy seated snugly in the upper basket, I took a sip of the latte I'd pick up on my way into the store. This had become our weekly ritual—indulging in retail therapy to fill the emptiness that had been gnawing at my insides since my husband left for the Middle East.

"We're getting extra money each month, deployment is hard, and I deserve a treat," I reasoned with myself. So far, the day's "treat" consisted of fancy coffee, new clothes, and a brightly colored educational toy that held my infant's attention for longer than two seconds. In the back of my mind, I knew that momentary rush of fulfillment accompanying fun purchases would only plug the void in my heart long enough to snip the price tag from each item.

Still, I wandered aimlessly through the aisles. As I made my way through the book section, a bright pink rectangle caught my eye—a Bible. Even though I already had one, it had been a while since I'd cracked it open. Maybe this pretty cover would encourage me to read? Sighing, I added it to the contents of my basket and turned toward the front of the store. "What's one more little thing?" I thought.

Moments later, I stood in the checkout line, staring in disbelief at the ugly word that had appeared on the screen: DECLINED. My cheeks flushed as I offered the cashier a flustered apology. Retrieving my phone from my purse, my fingers rushed frantically across the screen as I logged into our checking account and transferred money from savings. "That should do it," I said, holding my breath and keeping my eyes down as I swiped my debit card again. This time, a receipt appeared, and waves of hot guilt mixed with cooling relief. A rogue tear ran down my cheek as I made my way to the car. I was angry at myself, mad that I had been a poor steward of our finances and that I'd let our budget slip through my fingers.

I didn't start reading my new Bible right away. I was embarrassed, stubborn, and self-centered. However, God used my struggle to find peace in overspending and called me closer to him. That bright pink book was the best purchase I'd ever made.

As I developed a daily habit of savoring Scripture, my eyes began to open to the aching emptiness inside of me. Slowly, through prayer, personal devotions, and advice from trusted friends, I began to rely on the Holy Spirit to fill the void in every area of my life, including my finances. I learned that while earthly treasures may capture fragments of happiness like gold flakes in a sieve, God fills our inner void with true joy and peace as our faith grows.

How to Flourish in Not Overspending

1. **Acknowledge your finances belong to God.** Thank him for his provision, ask for forgiveness if necessary, and pray for wisdom and discernment in this area of your life.

2. **Seek wise advice and counsel.** Ask responsible friends, colleagues, and family members for a referral to a trusted financial advisor who can help you get back on track.

3. **Set a SMART (specific, measurable, attainable, realistic, and timely) goal.** Decide to pay off debt, save up for a family vacation, or boost your emergency funds.

4. **Create a plan.** Write out the steps you need to take to reach your financial goals and post them in a prominent spot.

5. **Surround yourself with people who will help you follow through with self-discipline.** If you slip up every once and a while, don't let it derail you. Find solid accountability partners and keep moving forward.

Flourish in Not Overspending

Verses to Consider

May the God of hope fill you with all joy and peace in believing, so that by the power of the Holy Spirit you may abound in hope (Romans 15:13).

Poverty and disgrace come to him who ignores instruction, but whoever heeds reproof is honored (Proverbs 13:18).

He who loves money will not be satisfied with money, nor he who loves wealth with his income; this also is vanity. When goods increase, they increase who eat them, and what advantage has their owner but to see them with his eyes? (Ecclesiastes 5:10–11).

Prayer

Lord, thank you for your mercy and faithful provision. Please help me to seek wisdom and discernment as I learn to flourish in my finances during deployment. Help me avoid overspending to stop up the emptiness I feel. Fill the void with your love, joy, peace, and hope. Amen.

28

Flourish in Moving

By Kori Yates

Sitting by the hotel pool watching my kids swim, I peruse the local rental housing market. It makes me chuckle that I am writing about how to flourish in times just like these. After packing out of our house in Germany, we traveled more than five thousand miles before settling in a new place.

This is not our first PCS rodeo. In fact, we are on number eight in our fifteen years of marriage. Each one different, and yet slightly the same. As we cruise through neighborhoods to get the lay of the land and find the house just right for us, we see everything from questionable apartments to pristine lawns that we can't afford. We do the same thing with churches, having moments when we wonder out loud whether we will make have friends in this new place.

A time of significant change can sometimes bring anxiety, fear, weariness, and a million other emotions we thought for sure we outgrew. It can be a challenging time, but it can also be a time of immense blessing—what I call a "Front row seat to see God at work."

During our first few moves, we started to see patterns of feelings—fear, anxiety, and weariness. Unwanted feelings showed up anyway. As schedule-oriented folks, this season of complete unknown unsettles us with the stress of transition.

But, God . . .

Then there was that one move where we started to see the bigger picture. It was a move to Georgia years ago when God showed up in an amazing way. At our previous duty station, we had given away furniture to a friend who was in need, anticipating we would replace it on the other end. We sold a house we had made "just right for us" to look for a rental we simply wanted to be habitable.

In Georgia, we looked at many houses to find a lot of nothing. It had gotten to the point that we didn't even get out and look in the windows anymore. Honestly, we were wondering if we could just live in the car. Then came THE house. We found our treasure. Just the right size with a price we could afford, it had the two pieces of furniture we had given away built into the house. The cherry on top? They had painted the master bedroom the same color as our previous house. It matched our comforter perfectly. Only

Flourish in Moving

God could do that. In that moment, our attitude toward moving changed forever.

This move gave us a tangible reminder of God. He had gone before us to choose a house, church, and friends that we would stay connected with for life. He brought blessings through jobs, neighbors and even landlords. We could not deny his presence or his provision. What we saw in this one tangible moment was what he had done multiple times before and has done many times since. He went before us and prepared the way. Having a plan just for us, not just in houses and neighbors, but also in our opportunity to make an impact right where we were. We had an "assignment"—one that was more than just orders on an email, but a greater assignment from the living God. He made a way for us to accomplish it.

We went from dreading moves to calling them our "Treasure Hunts" as we would go looking for all God would do in the place we were headed. Friends, houses, churches, and more were blessings God had already planned for us. They were treasures we looked to find, ways we could see God tangibly at work around us. We loved viewing moving as a "front row seat to see him at work." Looking for God changed our hearts, our perspectives, and our lives.

Our prayer is the one Moses prayed as the Lord asked him to lead the people of Israel into the Promised Land:

> *And he said to him, "If your presence will not go with me, do not bring us up from here. For how shall it be known that I have found favor in your sight, I and your people? Is it not in your going with us, so that we are distinct, I and your people, from every other people on the face of the earth?"* (Exodus 33:15–16).

It's kind of like saying, "I'll go if you go."

PCSing can still be hard and tiring, but our "Treasure Hunt" is one we hold dear. We would have missed this adventure if he had taken us on a different path in life. We have learned the grace of gratitude, even in the goodbyes and the starting overs.

How to Flourish during a Military Move

1. **Trust in God's character.** Throughout Scripture, God has made many promises to us about who he is and what he does. Trust that he is who he says he is. He is love. He is faithfulness. He is grace. He is hope. He is forever the same God.

2. **Go looking.** Good or bad we usually discover exactly what we seek. This PCS issue is no different. We must choose to go looking for God's provision and promise instead of dwelling on what we left behind. We will most likely find what we're looking for.

3. **Rest in his faithfulness.** Take a deep breath. This is a season. Soon enough you will have a church community in which to belong, friends to enjoy, and a place to call home. It takes time, but he is the God who provides.

4. **God has a plan for all of this.** Trust that God has a plan in every move, every assignment, every deployment, every TDY—all of it. We are missionaries accomplishing what God has sent us to do. He tells

us in Matthew 28:19–20: "Go therefore and make disciples of all nations, baptizing them in the name of the Father and of the Son and of the Holy Spirit, teaching them to observe all that I have commanded you. And behold, I am with you always, to the end of the age."

Verses to Consider

But you will receive power when the Holy Spirit has come upon you, and you will be my witnesses in Jerusalem and in all Judea and Samaria, and to the end of the earth (Acts 1:8).

Now the LORD said to Abram, "Go from your country and your kindred and your father's house to the land that I will show you" (Genesis 12:1).

Have I not commanded you? Be strong and courageous. Do not be frightened, and do not be dismayed, for the LORD your God is with you wherever you go (Joshua 1:9).

Prayer

Lord, I know you have gone before me and you go with me. As I start this new adventure, open my eyes to your work around me. Empower me to walk boldly in all you call me to do in this new place. Amen.

29

Flourish in Residency Change

By Jennifer Wake

MSRRA is a wonderful thing. However, few people know what it is. MSRRA stands for Military Spouses Residency Relief Act (Public law 111–97) passed in 2009. Doesn't that make everything perfectly clear? With the passing of this law, military spouses no longer pay income tax based on where their servicemember is stationed. Congress threw in a change to MSRRA on December 31, 2018. This change allows spouses to claim the same residency as their service member. This is a huge benefit.

Although both my husband and I claim New York as our state of residency, I have helped many spouses who were from states other than where the service member held their residency. Before this change many states taxed military spouses differently than military members. Now, spouses can choose to be from the state of their military member.

I call New York state home. Even though I moved every two years when I was little, I consider my home to be where my family finally settled. I still vote in New York through absentee ballots. My cars are registered in New York. I love being from Upstate New York.

I relate to the biblical women Naomi and Ruth. In the book of Ruth, Ruth decides to stay with Naomi after her husband dies. Leaving her home in Moab, Ruth follows Naomi back to the land of Judah.

> *But Ruth said, "Do not urge me to leave you or to return from following you. For where you go I will go, and where you lodge I will lodge. Your people shall be my people, and your God my God"* (Ruth 1:16).

Ruth chose to become a resident of Judah instead of Moab. In those times, people did not choose to leave their homelands. Ruth was still called a Moabite even though she moved away and gave up everything. She chose to go with Naomi out of love. Does that sound familiar? Many military spouses give up everything for love.

How to Flourish in the Residency Change

1. **Show your "home" pride.** Register your vehicles in the state where you hold your residency. It may be hard to return to the state to register your vehicle, but it shows you want to support your state. My plates start many conversations, usually it starts with "Are you from New York City?"

2. **Teach your kids about your "home."** My area of New York is known for the Women Suffrage movement. Teaching my children about that heritage is important to me.

3. **Pray while voting for your "home" officials.** Keep voting in your state of residency. Voting is one of our greatest rights. Along with voting, pray for your government leaders. Pray for them to lead wisely.

4. **Reflect on the story of Ruth in the Bible.** Ruth loved Naomi enough to move to a strange land. Naomi changed from bitter to loving because of Ruth's example. Study this story to learn about flourishing wherever God puts us.

Verses to Consider

And Peter said, "See, we have left our homes and followed you" (Luke 18:28).

Blessed are those who dwell in your house, ever singing your praise! (Psalm 84:4).

So Naomi returned, and Ruth the Moabite her daughter-in-law with her, who returned from the country of Moab (Ruth 1:22a).

Prayer

Lord, as I reflect on Ruth's choices let me be wise in my choices in the midst of transition and change. Help us to invest in our new community. Use us for your glory wherever you send us. Amen.

30

Flourish in Transition

By Kristin Goodrich

Twice during my Naval Service, I took off a set of uniforms for the final time. That finality triggers a range of emotions to this day. For my first four years I wore the uniforms of a Naval Academy midshipman. On the day I threw my cover into the air, half of my sea bag was no longer useful. The midshipman uniforms—dungarees for training, dress uniforms for drill, white works which we wore over PT gear, and more, all landed somewhere. I thought I had either donated or discarded all those uniforms.

Imagine my surprise when I found some of those long-forgotten uniforms in a box my dad gave me after my mom passed away. When I showed my young adult children a pair of "original" granny-panties, my kids were horrified! We had fun as I tried on the various uniforms. I could only button the choker collar of the drill jacket, but the white works jumper and bell-bottomed pants did fit, much to my delight. To my children's everlasting relief, I didn't model the granny-panties.

After four and a half years of service, I took off my military uniform. Now a dusty Ziploc bag holds insignia, ribbons, and medals, as well as the dog tags imprinted with my maiden name. As I touch each item, I reflect on my military experiences. I remember being at noon meal formation the day the Challenger space shuttle exploded. I can tell of learning about the Soviet fleet and watching the Berlin Wall fall. Also, many military friends have heard my "green T-shirt" story during which I was desperate to return to Panama in the proper uniform, prior to Operation Just Cause in 1989.

My time in service, represented by those uniforms and additional gear, was a narrative of sea stories—funny, heartbreaking, complex, and heartwarming. I've been challenged by the Holy Spirit to share these sea stories in ways that speak of God's awesome deeds in each of those military situations.

Throughout my military service, Psalm 139 was my favorite chapter in the Bible. When I was seasick during a North Atlantic storm and when I could feel the presence of evil in the jungles of Panama, these words strengthened my soul. Each of us can know as loved ones serve in sandboxes around the world, the Lord is always mindful of us. And for every situation in uniform—and every situation after we take off the uniform—God will lead us as followers of Jesus on the ultimate PCS journey. Thanks be to God for the privilege of wearing the military uniform, and for the responsibility to tell of his faithfulness across the generations. Sometimes, the stories of our transitions teach others to flourish, just as the experiences benefit us when they happen. How has God used transitions in your life?

How to Flourish in Transition

1. **Thank Jesus.** Look at your military experiences and thank Jesus for what you learned in the struggles and through the accomplishments.

2. **See God's presence.** Challenge yourself to see how God was ever-present across the miles and years.

3. **Tell others.** Share your stories with the next generation.

4. **Glorify God.** Make the Lord the HERO in your life story—during and after your time in uniform!

Verses to Consider

If I take the wings of the morning and dwell in the uttermost parts of the sea, even there your hand shall lead me, and your right hand shall hold me. If I say, "Surely the darkness shall cover me, and the light about me be night," even the darkness is not dark to you; the night is bright as the day, for darkness is as light with you (Psalm 139:9–12).

How precious to me are your thoughts, O God! How vast is the sum of them! If I would count them, they are more than the sand (Psalm 139:17–18a).

Search me, O God, and know my heart! Try me and know my thoughts! And see if there be any grievous way in me, and lead me in the way everlasting! (Psalm 139:23–24).

Prayer

Lord, we eagerly anticipate the day when we can share our sea stories with you in heaven. Guard the minds and souls of women currently wearing a military uniform. Encourage and strengthen those who have taken off their uniforms, whether by choice or by circumstance. Show us how you have been at work in our lives and how we might redeem our stories for your glory. Amen.

31

Flourish in Retirement

By Claudia Duff

When my husband retired from the Navy after twenty-three years it was sudden and unexpected. I wish I could say we were ready, but it took us by surprise, shaking us to the core. We enjoyed Navy life and the idea of doing something else was foreign to us. A bumpy change, it felt like riding on a rollercoaster with no safety bar.

But, God.

We couldn't see it yet, but God had a glorious plan for our lives. Living in the shadows of uncertainty, change weighed heavy on our hearts. Our transition took seven years and two jobs. I have learned that the circumstances of my life do not define the power of my God.

He is bigger, just flat out bigger, than being homeless, unemployed, and sick during the process of retirement. Okay, I'll tell this much: Within the first nine months of retirement, we were homeless for ninety days or so, my guy was unemployed for eight months, and I had major surgery (total hip replacement). That's a lot going on all at the same time. I was sure I wasn't going to survive that season, but here I am—still standing. I'm not just standing but standing in victory.

A friend gave me this verse: "He brought me out into a broad place; he rescued me, because he delighted in me" (Psalm 18:19).

When I shared what we were facing as a family, she just opened her Bible and read that Scripture rather than gush with sentiment or emotion. It was the best God encounter I have ever had. The words just screamed, "This is not an accident or even a mistake. I've got this and I am going to show you the blessings amidst this." This broad place was the unknown corner of our life, that God had yet to reveal. In the process God continued work in our lives. Many days it felt more like persecution than blessing. Psalm 18:19 strengthened me again and again. My prayer life began to flourish in this season of retirement, stirring a desire for more. As God carried us through the valley of retirement transition, he revealed some practical steps during my prayer time.

How to Flourish in Retirement

1. **Pray early.** Pray for times and places to begin a retirement discussion with your family.

2. **Share expectations.** Make a list of your family's expectations during the transition into retirement.

3. **Surround yourself.** Surround your family with people who will encourage you as well as offer sound, clear, and decisive advice.

4. **Pray always.** PRAY! PRAY! PRAY! Keep a prayer journal. It truly is a treasure to look back and see what God has done.

5. **Begin ASAP.** It is never too early to dream about life after the military. Make a short list of possible places to live and job opportunities long before your retirement date.

Like I said before, retirement has been a bumpy ride. Often, I felt like the light at the end of the tunnel was an oncoming train rather than deliverance from Jesus. Sometimes it was both. The train hit, but Jesus was right there to pick up the pieces of our shattered lives. We are somewhat settled in retirement life. Seven years later we have three high school graduates, one Bible college graduate, two college graduates, two daughters-in-love, three grandbabies, and one postgraduate degree. My guy loves his new job as a professor at a local university and I am over the moon that my town now has a Hobby Lobby!

No matter what you are facing, look up, because our Redeemer lives, and he lives in us. Retirement can be stressful for change is unsettling. But God is the ultimate settler of all things because he is the grand creator of all things. Look for Jesus in every circumstance of your retirement process, ask for help often, and pray always.

Verses to Consider

We are afflicted in every way, but not crushed; perplexed, but not driven to despair; persecuted, but not forsaken; struck down, but not destroyed; (2 Corinthians 4:8–9).

Blessed be the God and Father of our Lord Jesus Christ, the Father of mercies and God of all comfort (2 Corinthians 1:3).

Let your speech always be gracious, seasoned with salt, so that you may know how you ought to answer each person (Colossians 4:6).

Prayer

Lord, help me bless my family as we prepare to transition from the military into civilian life. Let us see you in the things we encounter, trusting you for every next step. Surround us with people who will lend a hand, support us through prayer, and give us encouragement as needed. Amen.

32

Flourish in The Best

By Kori Yates

I would volunteer for anything... literally. It's in my nature to help others. A survey USAA survey revealed 65-percent of people in the military community volunteer somewhere.

Of all the groups I have ever been a part of, the military community volunteers like none other. There could be multiple reasons for this, including the fact that jobs can be hard to come by for military spouses and they still want to use their skills. Maybe it is because we have learned to get involved quickly. Or maybe it's just that we are folks who volunteer. After all, some of us did sign up to wear a uniform. We volunteer—a lot.

Volunteering is good, really it is, but along the way sometimes we cross the line that separates brave from crazy. Have you been there? I have—more than once. Whether hosting a Bible study or coaching sports for children, I have a desire to step into almost any opportunity that comes my way. I either think, *It can't be that hard,* or *If I don't do it, it might not happen.* Hating to say no, I discovered that too many *yeses* started to overtake my life.

I can feel it inside when those good intentions and desires to serve cause anxiety in my heart. The stress of over-commitment overflows through words and actions to the lives I care about most. Not a pretty sight.

God wants me to do good works, but that doesn't mean I should say yes to every opportunity to serve. Obedience to him is the key. What does he want me to do? Whether I am busy or not, am I following Christ? Obedience helps me flourish and protects me from a crazy schedule.

How to Flourish in the Best

1. **Give it time.** When we move to a new location, we have a six-month rule. This is an agreement in our house that we will not make any long-term commitments in the first six months of a new duty station. We take time to pray and ponder how the Lord is working where we are and how he wants us to join him. The second is our accountability rule. Before agreeing to a volunteer commitment, my husband and I take time to talk with each other. This allows us to ponder, at least overnight, and gives us another perspective. If you don't have a spouse, find a good friend who will "give it to you straight."

2. **Determine your mission.** Stop and think about what God has taught you, what he has given you a passion for, and how you have used those giftings over the years. I have three general passions where I direct my time and energy: marriage, parenting, and military ministry. In pondering my volunteer time, I compare it to these things. If it doesn't line up, I take a hard look before jumping in.

3. **Recognize seasons.** As we move and grow, our mission, responsibilities, and time commitments change. We need to ask the question: What is needed in this season? I usually consider the state of our family (i.e., school ages for kids, deployments/TDYs expected, job commitments) as well as my personal state. How am I doing health-wise, spiritually, physically, and emotionally? These factor into the season I am in and can help determine what God would have me to do during this time.

God has a plan and purpose in every place he plants us. Seeking and being obedient to him is key. At the end of the day, I want my answer to be, "Sign me up!" to whatever God has called me to.

Verses to Consider

The saying is trustworthy, and I want you to insist on these things, so that those who have believed in God may be careful to devote themselves to good works. These things are excellent and profitable for people (Titus 3:8).

Let the one who is taught the word share all good things with the one who teaches. Do not be deceived: God is not mocked, for whatever one sows, that will he also reap. For the one who sows to his own flesh will from the flesh reap corruption, but the one who sows to the Spirit will from the Spirit reap eternal life. And let us not grow weary of doing good, for in due season we will reap, if we do not give up. So then, as we have opportunity, let us do good to everyone, and especially to those who are of the household of faith (Galatians 6:6–10).

For by grace you have been saved through faith. And this is not your own doing; it is the gift of God, not a result of works, so that no one may boast. For we are his workmanship, created in Christ Jesus for good works, which God prepared beforehand, that we should walk in them (Ephesians 2:8–10).

Prayer

Lord, show me your way. I long to do your will in this place, in this season. Help me to flourish in my obedience and trust you with the outcome. Amen.

33

Flourish in Hard Work

By Kristin Goodrich

*A*LL HANDS ON DECK FOR THE WORK PARTY?!?
Our military culture is full of contradictions and lingo. Just thinking of "mandatory fun," and the not-optional-by-any-stretch-of-the-imagination "work party," makes it easy to give NAVY the acronym of "Never Again Volunteer Yourself!"

At our house, we have regular "field days." Not the kind where you play outside with friends to earn blue ribbons but rather the kind that means sorting through last season's clothes, looking at piles of old papers, and deep cleaning the bathroom. Although my kids groan at our workdays, they develop camaraderie by working together.

When my Army friend, Barb, moved across town, Fulya, and I spent most of the day unpacking all the kitchen boxes and putting everything away. As we chatted, Fulya and

FLOURISH

I found the work easy and satisfying. Barb, on the other hand, felt like she had avoided the hardest and worst part of her move—unpacking the kitchen. Banding together to help a friend made the work for all of us lighter.

How to Flourish in Hard Work

Author Randy Frazee shares concepts from that help me flourish[5] when work is difficult.

1. **Start with a good night's sleep.** After creating Day and Night, the first day was described as "there was evening and there was morning" (Genesis 1:5). Even today, the Hebrew daily calendar starts with sunset, in contrast to our Western daily calendar starting with sunrise. What if we reordered our thinking and considered the previous night's sleep to be the "start of the day." I know that getting restful and adequate sleep sets me up for twelve hours of productivity during the day.

2. **Work hard during the day.** During the third through sixth days, God created plants, the heavens, animals, and man (Genesis 1:9–31). He gave them all work to do, in abundance, according to their design. When work feels "hard" I need to pause and pray that the

---

5 *Making Room for Life: Trading Chaotic Lifestyles for Connected Relationships*, Randy Frazee, 2003, Zondervan, Grand Rapids, Michigan 49530

Holy Spirit would clarify why the work feels difficult and show me purpose in it. Then I need to obey what God calls me to do.

3. **Make time for relationships.** According to Frazee, if we sleep for eight hours and work for twelve hours, we have four hours left at the end of the evening-day cycle. I know, I know. I can hear the military voices saying, "I get less than eight hours of sleep AND I have to work for more than twelve hours a day!" But dare we ask ourselves what are we doing instead of sleeping: electronics, worrying, caffeinated energy, or alcoholic buzz? Dare we ask ourselves what cutting back on work might mean: "lesser" achievement in man's world, not seeming to have it "all together" (whatever that looks like), or using work as a reason to avoid relationships needing our time and energy? Each one of us living this military life can make small decisions to keep sleep, work, and relationships in balance.

4. **Rest (also known as taking a Sabbath).** After hiking 14.5 miles in under six hours at an elevation close to two miles above sea level, the sport tracker app informed my buddy and me that our recovery time would be eight hours. Just like this new technology,

the military recognizes the need for rest by at times offering mid-tour R&R, casual status around holidays, and four-day weekends.

> Seventh day—*So God blessed the seventh day and made it holy, because on it God rested from all his work that he had done in creation* (Genesis 2:3).

Our bodies and our minds need time to rest for many reasons. I love waking up to a solution for a thorny issue after a good night's sleep. Giving myself time before and after our church/chapel services, as well as meeting with others during the week for prayer or Bible study, allows me to adjust my life navigational settings and headings. These benefits are available for you too.

May you be blessed beyond what you can ask or imagine as you sleep tight, work hard, and enjoy your relationships. I pray your productive days start with restful nights. So . . .

LIGHTS OUT IN ALL BERTHING COMPARTMENTS. MAINTAIN SILENCE ABOUT THE DECKS. GOODRICH OUT.

Verses to Consider

Therefore, my beloved brothers, be steadfast, immovable, always abounding in the work of the Lord, knowing that in the Lord your labor is not in vain (1 Corinthians 15:58).

Each one's work will become manifest, for the Day will disclose it, because it will be revealed by fire, and the fire will test what sort of work each one has done (1 Corinthians 3:13).

Do you see a man skillful in his work? He will stand before kings; he will not stand before obscure men (Proverbs 22:29).

Prayer

Lord, help me to embrace the rhythms you have designed throughout each day and each week. I need the Holy Spirit to lead me as I make decisions about sleep, work, and relationships. Amen.

34

Flourish in Balance

By Rachelle Whitfield

My side hustle is Marketing team lead for Planting Roots. By day I am a full-time Hospital Administrator. When I signed up to write this devotion several months ago. I must have been in one of those seasons when I had a little bit of confidence.

We had been at that duty station for two and a half years, so I had a system. I had a schedule at work, at home, and in ministry. I had friends, and it all ran like a well-oiled machine. Fast forward six months—I'm at a new duty station (no friends yet), setting up house (number eight in eleven years), and starting a new job. All of this before the old house was packed and the husband and dogs joined me. I know it sounds a little odd to be the one going ahead, since I am the spouse that usually follows my soldier.

Sometimes I think I have life figured out. At other times I am just praying that whoever saw me yesterday glimpsed Jesus in me and knows that he is the one who strengthens me, gives me drive, and forgives me when my shine is not so bright. I think the topic I officially chose to write about was "Flourishing in the Balancing of Faith and Work." As I considered this, I realized there is no balance to it. I tried to learn balance for many years and it just didn't work. I always leaned on one side of the fence or the other.

During one year, one duty station, and one new job, I decided I was going to act overtly as a Christian. I am a government employee, so I knew I could not be flamboyant. No camping out in the breakroom reading my Bible out loud hoping others received the Holy Spirit. Instead, I wanted to live in a way that my coworkers would see something different in me, drawing them to God through my attitude and actions.

But I got to talk about Jesus every day. I got to pray with and for people who weren't even sure what or who they believed in. And I got to share his Word with an amazing family who was never taught to read it on their own. Not only did I flourish personally, professionally, and spiritually, but I was loved well, and I learned to love well in kind. Only God could provide an opportunity like this. The best kind of balance comes when we seek to honor God in the way we live.

How to Flourish in Balance

1. **Establish a morning routine.** This is not just about "quiet time." Getting up early provides opportunity for an extra cup of coffee, to pack lunch, and prepare my work bag. Making time to read a short morning devotional and say a prayer to start my day is another part of my morning routine. With a little planning and discipline, I no longer crawl out of bed thirty minutes before I was supposed to be at my desk, trying to simultaneously brush my teeth, put on mascara, and find my keys.

2. **Find a community or group.** I'm blessed to have a couple of groups that hold a special place in my life—including my Planting Roots friends. I have never served alongside a group of women who get me, care about and appreciate my OCD, and accept my little rough-around-the-edges military style of communicating and thinking like they do. I also have my fitness friends that make working out fun, motivating me to drink water and eat healthy. I have a marriage community that inspires me to love my

husband well. The accountability of others helps me seek balance in important areas of life.

3. **Invest in your spiritual life.** I stay connected to a Christ-centered community that challenges me to grow in my spirituality. I need a pastor who notices I missed a couple of weeks and is bold enough to ask, "Where you have been?" I need a group of women who expect me to show up to Bible study, faithful to do the assignment and to participate in the discussion. God uses people to help maintain a balance that includes spiritual growth.

Some days I am exhausted, and some Sundays I don't want to leave my PJs because the weekend went by too fast. Many days I wonder if I have represented Christ well. However, I know he has me where I am for a purpose. That purpose is to represent him, whether through actions or words, and to flourish in and through him.

Verses to Consider

Go therefore and make disciples of all nations, baptizing them in the name of the Father and of the Son and of the Holy Spirit, teaching them to observe all that I have commanded you. And behold, I am with you always, to the end of the age (Matthew 28:19–20).

And whoever does not take his cross and follow me is not worthy of me. Whoever finds his life will lose it, and whoever loses his life for my sake will find it (Matthew 10:38–39).

But far be it from me to boast except in the cross of our Lord Jesus Christ, by which the world has been crucified to me, and I to the world (Galatians 6:14).

Prayer

Lord, thank you for showing me that balance is only possible with you. I may not find balance every day or in every place, but I know that the more time I spend with you the more balanced I feel. Help me to use my time and energy in a way that honors you. Amen.

35

Flourish in Housework

By Liz Giertz

I had a rude awakening when I took off my uniform after ten years of active duty. In military service my work seemed to matter. I moved heavy equipment off closing bases as we consolidated operations in Bosnia, managing the maintenance for a Battalion's worth of equipment, operating a military airfield for soldiers returning from war in Germany, and tracking transportation and logistics in Iraq. My superiors frequently commended me, their praise fed my ego and fueled my drive to continue performing at increasing levels.

Overnight, I went from briefing generals to bagging garbage, from giving orders to being a short order cook, from commanding troops to cleaning commodes. The work transition was hard and humbling. In uniform I was doing work the world noticed and valued, and then I wasn't.

There are no medals for toilet cleaning, sweeping, grocery shopping, or laundry folding. My effort was often unnoticed and felt unimportant in comparison to serving my country.

Housework is never finished. The toilets are one use away from needing another good scrub. Between the dog and the kids there are crumbs and fur on the floor before I get the mop hung back up in the closet. With two growing boys under our roof, we are usually only one bowl of cereal away from an empty box. The clothes I wear while folding will need to be washed tomorrow.

Popular culture sends the message that housework is beneath us women or that we are cheating ourselves by scrubbing floors and stocking the pantry. The world whispers that we could be making a huge impact, doing work that *really* matters, and that we deserve to be noticed and recognized for our contributions. Those messages only lead to bitterness and hostility in my home. When I believe that menial housework devalues my education and military experience, I need a new perspective. I remind myself of how God views the work I now do.

How to Flourish in Housework

1. **God sees my work.** Hagar, Sara's handmaid, referred to God with the title *El Roi, The God Who Sees*. She recognized that God saw her heart and the hardship she was enduring. Even when the work we do behind the scenes goes unnoticed by the world, God's Word assures us that he sees our effort.

2. **God values my work.** The Bible doesn't say "Cleanliness is next to godliness," but many of the commands outlined in the books of Exodus, Deuteronomy, Leviticus, and Numbers correlate to best practices for maintaining good health and cleanliness in the home and community. Nobody can accomplish work if a lack of cleanliness makes them sick. Proper hygiene keeps us all healthy and that is important to both me and God.

3. **God strengthens me for my work.** When the laundry piles high and there are more dishes piled in the sink than hours in the day to wash them, I remember that God is the One who gives me my strength. God

provides the hours in the day, the muscles in my arms and legs, the air in my lungs, and the will to go on when I would rather give up.

4. **God honors my work**. Jesus was very clear about the life he came to earth to live. He was committed to serving others for his Father's glory. God honors the humble, and it doesn't get much humbler than scrubbing toilets and floors on your hands and knees, except maybe the king of the universe dying on a cross for me. When my work humbles me, literally bringing me to my knees, I remember how Jesus humbled himself for me. I rejoice that God raised him up and seated him at his right hand.

When we accomplish work we would rather not do, simply for the good of others, we sacrifice for them. We posture our hearts to humbly honor others above ourselves. Sacrificing his life for ours. Jesus endured indescribable torture culminating in a criminal's death on the cross to fulfill God's just punishment for the sins of all mankind.

His sacrifice secured our salvation. When we sacrifice our dreams and desires to do unglamorous, yet necessary work for others, for a greater cause, we become more like Jesus. Following Jesus' example, I learn to see the value in doing all my work for his glory, whether military service or caring for my family. This helps me gain a heavenly perspective on housework.

When we remember that God sees, values, strengthens, and honors the humble, we discover that we can flourish doing anything—even scrubbing toilets.

Verses to Consider

And let us not grow weary of doing good, for in due season we will reap, if we do not give up (Galatians 6:9).

Whatever you do, work heartily, as for the Lord and not for men, knowing that from the Lord you will receive the inheritance as your reward. You are serving the Lord Christ (Colossians 3:23–24).

One's pride will bring him low, but he who is lowly in spirit will obtain honor (Proverbs 29:23).

Prayer

Lord, help me to remember that you not only see and value the work I do but you also strengthen me to serve others in my home. Give me a heavenly perspective on housework. Amen.

36

Flourish in Work

By Brenda Pace

My dad dropped out of school at a young age to work in the cotton mills of North Carolina. He worked hard to pull himself out of poverty by joining the Army and used his GI Bill to become the only person in his family to attend college. He eventually earned a PhD and was a successful college professor. Up until his death at age 89, he cared for my mother, kept a disciplined routine of home management, and found time to study and write every day. He worked hard throughout his life with a sense of enjoyment in his labor. I'm grateful for his example and legacy of diligence.

That example served me well at an age when many of my peers were retiring from their day jobs. After years of not bringing home a regular paycheck, I re-entered the paid workforce. The transition was not seamless (understatement), but whether paid or volunteer, I have never questioned the privilege granted me to do meaningful and purposeful work.

I heard a profound sermon on the topic of work. The preacher asked if we had heard or believed that work is a result of the fall of man and punishment for sin. He went on to declare that yes, work began in the garden of Eden, but man did not start to work after the fall, but before. *The Lord God took the man and put him in the garden of Eden to work it and keep it* (Genesis 2:15).

Toil and hardship in work came after the fall in Genesis 3:17, *. . . cursed is the ground because of you; in pain you shall eat of it all the days of your life.* Work is not a punishment—work is a gift from God. He created us in his image to work and care for his created order. He wants us to flourish in our work and enjoy the fruit of our labor which brings him glory.

How to Flourish in Work

In the book *Your Work Matters to God* authors William Hendricks and Douglas Sherman offer five purposes for work:

1. Through work we serve people.

2. Through work we meet our family's needs.

3. Through work we meet our own needs.

4. Through work we earn money to give to others.

5. Through work we love God.[6]

I am thankful for military personnel and military spouses who labor valiantly on behalf of our nation. On both sides of the uniform, military work matters to God. Those who with professional skill serve the nation, and with personal dedication serve God, have the elements of true fulfillment in work. Spouses who support and serve on the team share in a purposeful life that goes beyond a mere paycheck.

---

6 Doug Sherman, William Hendricks, *Your Work Matters to God* (Colorado Springs, CO: NavPress, 1987), 93.

Verses to Consider

There is nothing better for a person than that he should eat and drink and find enjoyment in his toil. This also, I saw, is from the hand of God (Ecclesiastes 2:24).

Behold, what I have seen to be good and fitting is to eat and drink and find enjoyment in all the toil with which one toils under the sun the few days of his life that God has given him, for this is his lot. Everyone also to whom God has given wealth and possessions and power to enjoy them, and to accept his lot and rejoice in his toil—this is the gift of God (Ecclesiastes 5:18–19).

For even when we were with you, we would give you this command: If anyone is not willing to work, let him not eat (2 Thessalonians 3:10).

Let the thief no longer steal, but rather let him labor, doing honest work with his own hands, so that he may have something to share with anyone in need (Ephesians 4:28).

Prayer

Lord, give me eyes to see my work as holy to you. May my work be an act of worship and may I do it heartily as to you. Amen.

37

Flourish in Intellectual Health

By Kristin Goodrich

I hate feeling dumb, and I hate looking dumb. I especially hated the feeling of looking dumb when I broke protocol as the first few notes of a military band echoed through a ceremony.

When in the military environment, we are trained to recognize the first few notes of traditional military music. In certain cases, such as the playing of the national anthem or the bugle rending of taps, we immediately stand at attention. Failing to correctly identify the first few notes of music played during an indoor military ceremony, I stood at attention while several hundred uniformed people in the room remained seated.

When I realized my mistake, I remained standing, having decided that sitting down would worsen my etiquette error. I could not wait for those excruciatingly long minutes to be over so that I could sit down or escape.

As soon as I could, I looked up the military regulations and discovered that I had indeed broken military protocol. Thankfully, in this case, my lack of military knowledge only resulted in embarrassment and a new desire to refresh my knowledge of military protocols.

My people are destroyed for lack of knowledge (Hosea 4:6a).

Just as knowledge is imperative on the job, fueling our minds with God's Word is a vital component of healthy faith. In the Bible, the Old Testament book of Hosea is full of God's instructions. To become smart about God's Word I need to move beyond the temptation to just read a few meme-worthy verses. Intellectual health is incomplete without a knowledge God's Word.

How to Flourish in Intellectual Health Through God's Word

1. **Read the whole text.** Take time to read the entire book of Hosea, which is less than ten pages long, or listen to an unabridged reading on audio. Regularly apply this principle by committing to a yearly Bible reading plan.

2. **Do some homework.** You may need to learn some vocabulary, spelling, pronunciation, and map locations to better understand what you are reading. For instance, in John 2:13, when Jesus spoke of "going up to Jerusalem," he had to walk uphill to get to the city. This information gives new insight to the text.

3. **Mix it up.** Refresh your "list of favorites" regularly by including a new devotional book, spend time in less familiar biblical passages, or try approaches such as journaling or writing out your prayers.

4. **Be critical.** Cultivate excellence as you develop critical thinking skills. Take time to become intellectually

disciplined as you ponder and reflect on the depth and breadth of God's Holy Word. Repeatedly, I have discovered and set aside false teachings because I took the time to measure great sounding ideas and well-delivered suggestions against Scripture according to 2 Timothy 3:16.

As I exercise my intellectual muscles and increase my knowledge base, my mind becomes more devoted to Christ. When I continue to exercise, my heart muscles engage and I become a more loving servant and shepherd, working in the military community for God's glory.

Over time and with increased experience and knowledge we generally move up in rank within the military community, whether we wear a uniform or not. In the military we become "old" when we enter our forties, whereas in civilian life, we become "old" decades later. Even though my service was short, local high school students have called me "an admiral or a general or something like that" because, to them, I'm old and have served.

However, age, experience, and knowledge do not necessarily equate to wisdom. Our purpose in cultivating intellectual health is to develop godly wisdom that we can lovingly share with our military sisterhood and the world around us.

Verses to Consider

Blessed is the one who finds wisdom, and the one who gets understanding (Proverbs 3:13).

Whoever is wise, let him understand these things; whoever is discerning, let him know them; for the ways of the LORD are right, and the upright walk in them, but transgressors stumble in them (Hosea 14:9).

And the child grew and became strong, filled with wisdom. And the favor of God was upon Him (Luke 2:40).

Prayer

Lord, help me to prioritize my intellectual health in many areas of life, but especially in my faith. Help me take time to read full passages in the Bible and to do some homework to better understand. Let me test what I learn and believe against your never-changing Word. Amen.

38

Flourish in Spiritual Health

By Muriel Gregory

"I can't eat that. My tape test is next week." My husband's diet often reflected whether he was about to take a PT test or if a tape test was on the calendar. The military ensures that its members are in top physical shape. The military culture is not alone in being obsessed with physical fitness.

From workouts to diets, skincare to vitamins, our culture is fascinated with self-care. The top pins on Pinterest are recipes and about looking our best. Beauty, fashion, and fitness are among the most popular blog topics. Unfortunately, our self-focused and surface-level society can undermine the benefits of inward, soul focus. Neglecting your spiritual health will have negative consequences.

Stress can lead to sleep disturbances, eating disorders, depression, anxiety, colds, and high blood pressure, to name a few. Madhukar H. Trivedi, M.D., wrote, "physical symptoms are common in depression, and, in fact, vague aches and pain are often the presenting symptoms of depression. These symptoms include chronic joint pain, limb pain, back pain, gastrointestinal problems, tiredness, sleep disturbances, psychomotor activity changes, and appetite changes."[7]

We discipline ourselves to stay on strict diets, and we train ourselves to run marathons, yet neglect to prepare for godliness. Let's change that.

> *Physical training is good, but training for godliness is much better, promising benefits in this life and in the life to come* (1Timothy 4:8 NLT).

---

[7] https://www.ncbi.nlm.nih.gov/pmc/articles/PMC486942/

How to Flourish in Spiritual Health

1. **Be humble.** "Humility is not thinking less of yourself, it's thinking of yourself less.[8]" The wisdom of Rick Warren has removed the stress of performance, the need to impress others, and the striving to outdo somebody else. When my focus is God and God alone I feel at peace.

2. **Be thankful and content.** Thankfulness breeds contentment, which in turn leads to more thankfulness. When we practice gratitude, we focus on what we have versus what we want. Consumerism will lead you to believe that you do not have enough, when the reality is we are affluent people. Our basic needs are met and most of our wants covered. Being thankful is good for your soul.

3. **Practice self-control.** I don't know about you, but I struggle with this one. Self-control is necessary for good health because it can prevent you from eating another cookie or the whole bag of chips. It can

---
8 Rick Warren, *The Purpose-Driven Life: What on Earth Am I Here For?* (Grand Rapids: Zondervan, 2002), 170.

alleviate the urge to spend hours on Facebook or Pinterest. So how do you practice self-control? Paul's advice can help you with that: "So, whether you eat or drink, or whatever you do, do all to the glory of God" (1 Corinthians 10:31).

4. **Be kind and gentle.** Put on kindness and gentleness before deciding on your outfit for the day. Pray for those to be evident in your life. Billy Graham defined gentleness as "sensitive regard for others and is careful never to be unfeeling for the rights of others."[9] "Since God chose you to be the holy people he loves, you must clothe yourselves with tenderhearted mercy, kindness, humility, gentleness, and patience" (Colossians 3:12 NLT).

5. **Pursue joy.** Joy is not a manufactured emotion. Pure joy is not found when everything seemed to go your way and you just had the best day of your life. Instead, joy is a manifestation of the Spirit inside of you. Turn your focus on what brings God pleasure, and joy will manifest in your heart. "For the joy of the Lord is your strength" (Nehemiah 8:10b).

---

9 Quoted in a sermon at https://sermons.faithlife.com/sermons/471988-gentleness

Flourish in Spiritual Health

6. **Find peace.** Peace is not the absence of chaos and suffering. Rather, it is best found amid them. "Don't worry about anything; instead, pray about everything. Tell God what you need, and thank him for all he has done" (Philippians 4:6 NLT).

7. **Love.** Love first, love second, love always. Love boldly and with all abandonment. Love without prejudice or borders. Love because He first loves you (1 John 4:19). Love because it is the greatest commandment (Matthew 22:37–39). Love because everything is meaningless without love (1 Corinthians 13).

Verses to Consider

Be not wise in your own eyes; fear the Lord, and turn away from evil. It will be healing to your flesh and refreshment to your bones (Proverbs 3:7–8).

My son, be attentive to my words; incline your ear to my sayings. Let them not escape your sight; keep them within your heart. For they are life to those who find them, and healing to all their flesh (Proverbs 4:20–22).

Gracious words are like a honeycomb, sweetness to the soul and health to the body (Proverbs 16:24).

Prayer

Lord, I thank you for your love and guidance. I am amazed at how you care about every aspect of my life. Let your light continue to guide me in the process of growing in spiritual health. Amen.

39

Flourish in Frustration

By Kelli Baker

In life, we all face situations that propel our minds and thoughts on a roller coaster of emotions. How do we get off the ride when we feel ourselves spiraling and lost in these thoughts? It is essential to recognize the thought that begins the roller coaster ride. In 2 Corinthians 10:5, Paul teaches us to "take captive every thought to make it obedient to Christ." To flourish during frustration, we need a plan of action to implement when frustrated thoughts and feelings tempt us for another ride.

In the military, there are many opportunities to exercise the skill of taking every thought captive. The different personalities we encounter along the way can cause frustration and friction within a team. A leader may make a decision we don't feel is the best for the team. How often do we find ourselves in hot water when we don't stop and think before we speak, allowing our words to get the best of us? Instead, capturing that thought and holding our tongue is probably the best decision one could make in that situation. When we are mindful of the thought to begin with, we have the opportunity to gather our thoughts and formulate a plan of action to approach the leader one-on-one to air our grievances. Not seeing eye-to-eye on something can be very frustrating, but even more so, our reputation is on the line when we allow our uncaptured thoughts to rule our speech.

Remaining mindful and observant of your thoughts is the first step. Making it a priority to be present and recognize when these thoughts pop into your head is key. Meditating on scripture is an excellent way to practice this skill. Then, decide what you will do with these thoughts and feelings when they arise.

How to Flourish in Frustration

1. **Be still and wait patiently for the Lord to intervene.** (Psalm 37:7) If you can just stop whatever you are doing and take some deep breaths, you will allow space for God to enter and speak to you in his small still voice.

2. **Think about the positive things in these situations.** (Philippians 4:8) In the middle of frustration, it can be difficult to not focus on what is annoying you. However, shifting your focus can help you respond in a more productive manner. One example is how I deal with my very emotional and passionate son. At the time of this writing, he was almost six, tended to overreact about mundane things, and would go into a tailspin of anger and frustration. If I am not present and conscious of my thoughts I can get caught up in emotions, focusing only on the negative behavior. Instead, when I shift my focus to the true, noble, pure, and admirable aspects of my son or the situation, I am better equipped to handle it as God would have me. Numerous times we read in the Bible that God is slow to anger and rich in love. Isaiah 12:1

shows us an example of how God turned his anger away and responded with comfort. The ESV version says it like this: "For though you were angry with me, your anger turned away that you might comfort me." Thinking about the goodness in the situation can help change your thought pattern and get you off the nasty emotional roller coaster in your thoughts.

3. **Respond with kind words.** (Proverbs 16:24) It is so easy to lash out and respond with mean and hurtful words when sinful thoughts spiral in our heads. However, we can become more like Christ when we are able to respond with kindness. The Bible talks about the power of the tongue. Proverbs 18:21 says that "Death and life are in the power of the tongue." In Proverbs 16:24 (NLT), it says, "Kind words are like honey, sweet to the soul and healthy for the body." When you respond with kind words you are helping to build others up rather than crush their spirit. So, when you feel overwhelmed and burdened by your thoughts, stop and take a moment to reconnect with the Father. Think on the goodness of the situation, then respond with kind words and celebrate, knowing that God is strengthening you in times of frustration.

Verses to Consider

Be still before the Lord and wait patiently for him; fret not yourself . . . (Psalm 37:7).

May the God of hope fill you with all joy and peace as you trust in him, so that you may overflow with hope by the power of the Holy Spirit (Romans 15:13 NIV).

Finally, brothers, whatever is true, whatever is honorable, whatever is just, whatever is pure, whatever is lovely, whatever is commendable, if there is any excellence, if there is anything worthy of praise, think about these things (Philippians 4:8).

Prayer

Lord, fill me with your hope, joy, and peace, especially when I am frustrated. Teach me to trust in you more so that I may overflow with hope and forever be found flourishing, despite my feelings, by the power of your Holy Spirit. Amen.

40

Flourish in Physical Health

By Kori Yates

After college, I participated with a sports mission trip to Madagascar. In my early twenties, I lived in the moment with little intentionality or discipline in my life. I raising money for my trip, but I did not make any other preparations.

During our second day we took a bus ride to a remote part of the island. Our vehicle overheated and everybody on our team got sick. Not car sick but eat-the-wrong-food-only-been-in-country-two-days kind of sick. Everyone on our team except me.

Arriving at our destination, we had just hours before we played our first game. Nobody was well by game time. Being the only one not sick, I ended up playing the entire game while everyone else substituted frequently. By the fourth quarter we had to call timeouts just so I could breathe. It was a fast-paced, hour-long game which I was not physically ready to play. I know you may be thinking it is totally understandable to not be able to sprint for that long, but God taught me a powerful lesson. In my exhaustion, God spoke to my heart, saying, "Kori, you say you want to serve me and yet you don't take the time or make it a priority to prepare yourself to do so."

It hit home, for sure. God taught me that keeping myself healthy and my body strong was an important aspect of ministry. How was I going to serve him to the best of my ability if I wasn't physically prepared?

Physical health is more than physical fitness and good nutrition. It is also a matter of worship. This lesson prepared me to be ready when God prompted me to join the Marine Corps. Without the years of physical training that resulted from the desire to honor God with my physical health, I wouldn't have had the confidence to step into the physical rigor of military life.

Physical health varies for all of us because our bodies are all different. You may be a marathoner or a water aerobics advocate. Maybe you love group fitness classes. What about a morning walk or a ride on a stationary bike? One of those may be just what you're looking for. There are any number of ways to keep active and healthy. Good stewardship of our bodies includes exercise. Find what works for you and do it regularly.

Some of us have reasons we cannot do certain things, whether through physical limitations, illnesses, etc. Physical fitness isn't a contest. It is an act of worship—taking the body God has given us and doing our very best with it. If I am going to serve the Lord with all my might or strength, I want to give the very best in worship to him.

How do I grow in this area? As the years pass, I have found my physical needs change. Marriage, kids, jobs, etc., all influence this area. What does the Lord want it to look like for this season? He has a plan for our physical health and well-being.

How to Flourish in Physical Health

1. **Make it a habit.** This is vital to my success. If I don't put it on the schedule and make it part of my routine it won't ever happen.

2. **Add variety.** Doing the same thing every day can make us and our bodies bored. Try different types of exercise in your routine to add variety.

3. **Bring friends or meet new friends.** Exercising with friends or a group can make a difference. When I know someone is waiting for me, I tend to show up a lot more regularly. It certainly helps to have accountability.

4. **Consume wisely.** Being healthy is not just about what exercise you're doing. It also includes what you take into your body. Not sure? Make a food journal. Keeping track of what you eat may surprise you.

5. **Be you.** This is your reminder that we are not all created the same. God desires that we use what he has given us to the best of our ability. This is not a comparison game.

God has given me this one life. My goal is to make it count—to be as ready as possible when he asks me to do something. How are you staying ready? In what ways do you need to grow healthier so you can fully flourish as you serve God?

Verses to Consider

Or do you not know that your body is a temple of the Holy Spirit within you, whom you have from God? You are not your own, for you were bought with a price. So glorify God in your body (1 Corinthians 6:19–20).

So, whether you eat or drink, or whatever you do, do all to the glory of God (1 Corinthians 10:31).

You shall love the LORD your God with all your heart and with all your soul and with all your might (Deuteronomy 6:5).

Prayer

Lord, remind me that all I have is yours. I pray for the courage and commitment to use it all for your glory. This is my act of worship. Amen.

41

Flourish in Remembering

By Jennifer Wake

My family loves to celebrate. As a military family, we've discovered that remembering to celebrate is great way to build continuity in our transitory lifestyle. With food and friends, we celebrate birthdays, anniversaries, the Super Bowl, March Madness, the Stanley Cup, Thanksgiving, Memorial Day, the World Series, and the list goes on. One of my friends celebrates birthdays and "Gotcha Days" (the day of their child's adoption) for everyone in their family with ice cream for breakfast. Now that is celebration taken seriously.

We celebrate so often that I forgot a very important day in each of our child's lives, their "Rebirth" day. That is the day they accepted Christ as their savior. I need my photo albums to recall the exact date of their baptisms. Remembering these spiritual milestones is a way of celebrating what God has done in our family. To me, these are important days to commemorate.

In the Old Testament, God reminded the people of Israel to remember his faithfulness through celebration. In Leviticus 23, the Lord commanded the Israelites to gather all the produce of the land to offer sacrifices to him, and to build temporary shelters (booths) to live in seven days. This celebration, known as the Feast of Booths, called for rest on the first and eighth day. They had to rest before and after the huge celebration. The days in between are full of celebration of what God provided in the harvest. This celebration also reminds his people of their journey in the desert and how God blessed them.

> *On the fifteenth day of the seventh month, when you have gathered in the produce of the land, you shall celebrate the feast of the LORD seven days* (Leviticus 23:39a)

In Luke 15, Jesus told the Parable of the Prodigal son. After the youngest son (the Prodigal) returns, the father commands everyone to celebrate and orders the fattened calf to be slaughtered for the great feast. This father does not give a small party. He gives an over-the-top party to celebrate his child's return. Think of it as having the best

Flourish in Remembering

meal every day for a month, or ice cream for breakfast for a week. This celebration is to remember the return of the son who was lost.

> *'And bring the fattened calf and kill it, and let us eat and celebrate. For this my son was dead, and is alive again; he was lost, and is found.' And they began to celebrate* (Luke 15:23–24).

We are all called to remember and celebrate God's faithfulness. In what ways do you celebrate God's faithfulness through remembrance? Do you eat too much food? Dance? Tell Stories? One of our favorite family celebrations come during the Christmas season. We remember the whole year of God's care for us. We love to spend time remembering how God brought us through the bad times, and the ways he has blessed us in the good ones. Remembering what God has done gives us much to celebrate!

How to Flourish in Remembering

1. **Journals.** Write down how God has provided for you each day. Think about both the big things and little things. Sometimes just having help to get through a trying day is cause for celebration. (Exodus 34:27)

2. **Stones.** The Israelites built altars and memorials to help them remember. He also gave them festivals to remember what he provided. After they crossed the Jordan, men had to go back to get stones from the center of the river to remember the miracle God performed. Set up stones of your own, either real stones of remembrance, or virtual ones that remind you of God's care. (Deuteronomy 27:1–8)

3. **Pictures.** My in-laws write stories on the back of picture frames to remember who was with them and where they were when the picture was taken. God uses the rainbow to paint the sky to remember the story of Noah What images will you use for remembrance? (Genesis 9:15–16)

4. **Stories.** Tell your faith stories. God, through Moses, commanded the Israelites to tell the story of the Passover, every year, to highlight his care for them. (Exodus 13:1–16). When God shows his faithfulness to you, enjoy telling the story of what he has done.

Verses to Consider

And the LORD said to Moses, "Write these words, for in accordance with these words I have made a covenant with you and with Israel" (Exodus 34:27).

And on the day you cross over the Jordan to the land that the LORD your God is giving you, you shall set up large stones and plaster them with plaster. And you shall write on them all the words of this law, when you cross over to enter the land that the LORD your God is giving you, a land flowing with milk and honey, as the LORD, the God of your fathers, has promised you (Deuteronomy 27:2–3).

I will remember my covenant that is between me and you and every living creature of all flesh. When the bow is in the clouds, I will see it and remember the everlasting covenant between God and every living creature of all flesh that is on the earth (Genesis 9:15–16).

Prayer

Lord, thank you for your faithfulness in my life. Thank you for your protection, your guidance, your help, and your provision. Teach me to remember and to celebrate your faithfulness. Amen.

42

Flourish in Celebration

By Kori Yates

Giving gifts is not one of my strengths and remembering special dates is a challenge for me. I have friends and family who are good at both. They know just the right gift for just the right occasion. They faithfully call or text on the exact day of birthdays. Thinking about my lack of skill in these areas could frustrate or disappoint me, but it doesn't. I have learned the importance of celebrating—whether it's the perfect gift, a needed reminder from Facebook, or just showing up.

Celebration is good.

We have many opportunities in military life to celebrate. From promotions to job changes, and babies to weddings, ceremonies abound, as does the cake. In addition to the many military festivities, I discovered the importance of celebrating the smaller moments just as much as the larger ones.

The pomp and circumstance of ceremonies, the joy of new births, and new lives joined in matrimony are occasions worth celebrating. However, completing a challenging schools, reaching a new rank, or finding a new house at a new duty station are important milestones to recognize. In our family, we have even celebrated finding our way around our new location without the GPS, going a bit farther down the trail on our run, or making new friends. These celebrations don't require balloons and gifts, but they are still moments to commemorate.

On our fifteenth wedding anniversary, my husband and I planned to go out to dinner. Still unpacking from a move, we enjoyed the simplicity of good food and good conversation at a nearby restaurant. While we were gone, our children worked hard to surprise us. When we arrived home, they ushered us into the living room where our wedding picture was posted on one of the moving boxes. There were two hearts and a hand-crafted sign hanging from the landing at the top of the stairs. We looked up to see our kids shower us with homemade confetti as they shouted, "Happy Anniversary!" What a special memory!

I love these recognitions. The spontaneous joy and heart-felt sentiments make it special. God has truly given us reason to rejoice because blessings abound in our lives. I have found that happy observances begin with thankfulness.

Reflect gratitude for things others have done, as well as for the blessings of God. The Bible is packed with festivals and remembrances. Reading through the Old Testament, it becomes obvious that celebration is important to God. He commands the Israelites to observe many feasts. I think he has several purposes in the commands to celebrate:

1. Gratitude for the goodness of God.

2. Remembering what God has done.

3. Honoring God with sacred observance.

Celebration is important for us because it's important to God. In our family, we've gotten better at recognizing special moments, but it takes intention and practice.

How to Flourish in Celebration

1. **Start with giving thanks**. A heart of thankfulness cannot help but recognize what the Lord has done.

2. **Join with others.** Sharing the blessings of the Lord benefits us and those with whom we share. It spurs us all on. (Hebrews 10:25)

3. **Simple is good.** Celebrations don't always have to include gifts and food. Sending a card, giving a high five, or sharing a story are simple ways to cheer and bless others.

4. **Take it home.** Sometimes we celebrate more with the people outside our house than we do the people inside. God has done great works inside the four walls of our homes. Make a point to develop your own family celebrations.

Flourish in Celebration

Verses to Consider

And let us consider how to stir up one another to love and good works, not neglecting to meet together, as is the habit of some, but encouraging one another, and all the more as you see the Day drawing near (Hebrews 10:24–25).

Rejoice always, pray without ceasing, give thanks in all circumstances; for this is the will of God in Christ Jesus for you (1 Thessalonians 5:16–18).

And when those who bore the ark of the LORD had gone six steps, he sacrificed an ox and a fattened animal. And David danced before the LORD with all his might . . . (2 Samuel 6:13–14).

Prayer

Lord, help me celebrate all you have done today, to share with others the blessing of you, because truly the "joy of the Lord is my strength" (Nehemiah 8:10). Amen.

43

Flourish in Celebrating Like Jesus

By Muriel Gregory

Come to the table.

Growing up, the Sunday meal was my favorite time of the week. Raised in France, food represented something close to our daily religion. The Sunday meal, a two to three-hour affair, was filled with delicious food, lively conversation, good wine, and the lingering feeling that, maybe, just maybe, this was simply perfection.

Beautiful things happen when people come around a table. Since moving to the United States, my favorite holiday has become Thanksgiving. It reminds me of Sunday meals in France. I can honestly say the military ensured that no two Thanksgivings resembled each other. Sometimes we hosted twenty people, other times it was just the kids and me. We have celebrated Thanksgiving with snow on the ground and in eighty-degree weather.

Much of Jesus' ministry happened around food and celebration. When he came to the table everyone was invited. Nobody was left out because of poor life choices or low social status. Jews and Gentiles, Pharisees and tax collectors, synagogue goers and prostitutes, all were welcome at his table. Jesus transformed a simple meal into an invitation to his kingdom.

Imagine him saying to you, "Come all you who are weary, come to the table and sit with me. Come and receive from me. Receive and be satisfied." In the Bible, Jesus tells us:

"I am the bread of life" (John 6:48).

"Everyone who drinks of this water will be thirsty again, but whoever drinks of the water that I will give him will never be thirsty again. The water that I will give him will become in him a spring of water welling up to eternal life" (John 4:13–14).

The early church understood the importance of the fellowship that happens around a table. They would gather, eat, and pray together (Acts 2:42). The writer of Hebrews urges us not to stop meeting together (Hebrews 10:25).

Come to the table. Do you hear Christ's call?

Flourish in Celebrating Like Jesus

This invites us to partake in Jesus' life and ministry. Come to the table and invite others to join you. Often this military life takes us away from those whom we know to be family. Invite others to come to your table and celebrate the joy of fellowship like Jesus. In the process you will make new friends. Some will become like family to you.

How to Flourish in Celebrating Like Jesus

1. **Gather with other believers.** Jesus will naturally join you (Matthew 18:20).

2. **Do not worry too much about the food and decoration.** Create an inviting atmosphere, and most of all, do it all for the glory of God (1 Corinthians 10:31).

3. **Show hospitality to strangers.** Consider that new family on post or that neighbor you have not met yet. Beautiful things happen when we entertain strangers (Hebrews 13:1–2).

4. **Turn your table into a sanctuary.** Make it a place of no judgment, a haven where all are heard and celebrated (Matthew 7:1).

5. **Celebrate and love one another.** Jesus gave us a new commandment to love one another. (John 13:34).

Flourish in Celebrating Like Jesus

So, gather around the table and linger there. Let a simple meal turn into a celebration. Tune the world out, and as you celebrate with friends and family, pause and notice the peace and joy found there. Then you will know the truth that Jesus is present as well.

Verses to Consider

"For where two or three are gathered in my name, there am I among them" (Matthew 18:20).

And they devoted themselves to the apostles' teaching and the fellowship, to the breaking of bread and the prayers (Act 2:42).

Let brotherly love continue. Do not neglect to show hospitality to strangers, for thereby some have entertained angels unaware (Hebrews 13:1–2).

Prayer

Lord, I thank you for the fellowship of believers. I thank you for the example set by your son. I am grateful for the opportunity this season to invite others to come to the table with me and partake in a simple celebration of life. Amen.

44

Flourish in Difficult Holidays

By Liz Giertz

Sometimes holidays stress me out.

Military life can bring challenges to holidays and family celebrations. As military women, we know the ache of deployments, countless delays, mixed up duty rosters, training exercises, or the lack of leave days causing missed special occasions. Even the threat of a pending hardship tour can put a damper on the best celebration.

Travelling long distances to spend short periods of time with loved ones we rarely see is exhausting. One year we spent a holiday huddled in a corner of the airport taking turns guarding our luggage with two small children sleeping on USO provided cots. When traveling for holidays is just too hard, we bear the guilt of not being present. We feel disappointment when limited time makes meaningful connections impossible.

To make matters worse, the military world often chides, "Suck it up buttercup. You knew what you signed up for." Truly, none of us know how hard military life is until we live it. Challenges change with each duty station, every added responsibility, and the many seasons of life. None of us know the extent of the expectations the military or our loved ones will place on us until they become too heavy to bear on our own. Celebrations and holidays can prove some of the hardest times for military families.

Flourish in Difficult Holidays

How to Flourish in Spite Of

1. **Give yourself permission to feel what you feel.** Your feelings are valid and they can be good indicators of your heart condition, but you don't have to wallow in them. Feel them and find God's truth in your situation.

2. **Establish healthy boundaries and practice soul care.** When life got hard Jesus got away by himself to commune with the Father. It is perfectly acceptable to get away and pray and read your Bible or call a mentor when the stress gets overwhelming. You can say no to people, situations, and expenses that add stress to your life.

3. **Look for what God is doing in this situation.** God is always at work. There has never been a time when he was not motivated by love with a purpose of redemption. When we train ourselves to look for what he might be doing in our difficult situations, we begin to see his hand in everything, a cause for celebration.

4. **Remember what you are really celebrating.** When you start to see God's hand at work in your difficult and stressful situations you'll never be at a loss for something to celebrate. In the Old Testament, God instituted the feasts for the Israelite people. He wanted his people to remember and celebrate what he had done for them. When we remember God's past faithfulness, we find the faith to flourish in the present and the courage to step forward into every tough assignment.

5. **Serve someone else.** When we serve someone else it takes the focus off ourselves. Becoming others-focused can minimize our own problems and remind us of all we have to celebrate.

The truth is, we are not always going to feel like celebrating just because a certain day on the calendar rolls around. When we make celebrating God's past faithfulness a way of life, when we incorporate it into everything we do, we will find ways to flourish even when we don't feel festive.

Flourish in Difficult Holidays

Verses to Consider

Weeping may tarry for the night, but joy comes with the morning (Psalm 30:5b).

Blessed be the Lord, who daily bears us up; God is our salvation (Psalm 68:19).

May the God of hope fill you with all joy and peace in believing, so that by the power of the Holy Spirit you may abound in hope (Romans 15:13).

Prayer

Lord, help me to always celebrate your faithfulness even when I don't feel festive, so that I might have the opportunity to share my joy with others. Amen.

45

Flourish in Identity

By Liz Giertz

When I got out of the Army, exchanging my active duty ID card for a "dependent" card was hard. Being a soldier defined my existence for more than two decades. From the time I was eight years old I dreamed of attending West Point and serving my country. That desire motivated me to take hard classes, make good grades, seek leadership roles, excel at sports, participate in extracurricular activities, and stay out of trouble—for the most part. When I put on the uniform I did what good soldiers do, and I was rewarded for it.

However, when I took off the uniform, I had no idea who I was anymore. Even though already a mother and a wife, I struggled to find my new identity out of uniform. It is a dangerous thing to try to determine our own identity because too often what we identify with becomes an idol in our lives. I didn't understand then that just because I had carried an active duty military ID card, soldier wasn't really my identity. There is a distinct difference between identity and vocation.

The world loves labels, telling us that what we do is who we are. Tragically, all the labels we wear, the cards we carry, the things we do, could all be gone tomorrow. Basing our identity on what we do is like building on a foundation of sand—tenuous and temporary. Our eternal identity was determined by our Creator before we were even conceived.

Who we think we are has a lot of power over what we do. To flourish in life, we need understand our identity. One of my favorite stories in the Bible highlights this concept.

David, anointed as the next King of Israel, was on the run from Saul, the current king. David and his men had been providing protection for a rich man's property and asked to be allowed to participate in a feast. The rich man foolishly refused, and for lack of a better term, it was as if David forgot who God had said he was.

David hastily planned an attack on the man's property, his people, even his life, as revenge for this apparent slight. Thankfully the rich man's wife, Abigail, gathered supplies and ran out to meet David and his men. She apologized for her husband's poor behavior and reminded David

Flourish in Identity

of his own identity. She told him he would not want the guilt of this blood on his hands when he became king and begged him to reconsider. David relented. God struck the rich man. The man died. And Abigail became David's wife. Remembering who he was had the power to change David's behavior (1 Samuel 25).

What we believe about our identity impacts our actions as well:

When we believe we are new creations in Christ we begin to say and do things that reflect our true identity.

When we believe we are children of God we trust him at his Word and depend on Him for provision.

When we believe we are temples of the Holy Spirit we begin to treat our bodies accordingly.

When we believe we are holy and set apart to honor God we act that way.

When we believe we are loved and forgiven, we can love and forgive others.

When we believe we are made in God's image we look for ways to be more like him.

When we believe we are citizens of an eternal kingdom we begin to set our minds on things that will outlive us.

But . . . if we put what we do before who we are and we fall short, we question our identity. Flourishing in faith comes as we embrace our identity in Christ.

How to Flourish in Identity

1. **Remember who God says you are.** God is the one who made each of us holy and beloved in Christ. We must constantly remind ourselves of this fact so we can focus on transforming into his image rather than conforming to the world's standards of success.

2. **Work from your identity, not to form it.** We think we must work to display our worth, but we are already valuable because God paid for us with his son Jesus' blood. Knowing who we are enables us to derive more pleasure from what we do and minimizes the pain when we can't do it anymore.

3. **Find your 'Abigail.'** Surround yourself with people, or even one close friend, who will remind you of who you are and then be humble enough to accept their redirection.

Instead of finding our identity in our vocation, we thrive when we live from our God-given identity. Military women, in or out of uniform, flourish by faith when they find their identity in Christ.

Verses to Consider

But he who is joined to the Lord becomes one spirit with him (1 Corinthians 6:17).

But you are a chosen race, a royal priesthood, a holy nation, a people for his own possession, that you may proclaim the excellencies of him who called you out of darkness into his marvelous light (1 Peter 2:9).

I have been crucified with Christ. It is no longer I who live, but Christ who lives in me (Galatians 2:20a).

Prayer

Lord, help me to tear down any idols I have created because of what I do. Teach me to find security in the identity you have given me so that I may flourish by faith. Amen.

Conclusion

By Kori Yates

I don't want to simply survive.

Military life can bring its own set of challenges. I totally get it. From deployments to field training, and test flights to PCSs, we walk through some tough situations. Listening to those around me and even hearing words from my own mouth, I sense us many times wishing or wanting things to be easier instead of walking in faith.

Amid the hard and difficult, the weary and sad, we can get caught up in wishing for what we left behind or wanting something more. We say things like:

"When this deployment is over, I'll . . ."

"At our next duty station, I'll . . ."

"When I retire, I'll . . ."

Sometimes these words can signal goals we are working to achieve or activities dependent upon certain locations or circumstances. However, I think often they are our way of putting off what God has called us to simply survive the place where we live.

I have totally been there.

But I believe God has something more for us than simple survival. He wants us to flourish, which means to grow, thrive, increase, and bloom.

Flourish today, in the place where you find yourself, not in some unknown place down the road at some undesignated time. Walk in the strength, hope, and freedom that only comes from him.

At Planting Roots we have attempted to dig into just that. How do we flourish where we are today? How do we thrive during trips to the sandbox or out on the ocean? How do we find joy despite crazy parenting or difficult marriages? How do we bloom when friendships constantly change and transitions are a normal part of life? How do we increase our prayer lives, work/volunteer activities, or health? How do we flourish in all of it?

Difficult questions when we're smack in the middle of hard.

Our main flourish verse has been Psalm 92:12–13:

Flourish in Identity

> *The righteous flourish like the palm tree and grow like a cedar in Lebanon. They are planted in the house of the LORD; they flourish in the courts of our God.*

In Christ we can flourish in the arid desert just as much as in the fertile fields. God has more for us than barely making it from day to day. As we close out this book on flourishing and look forward to the good fruit God is growing in us, we encourage you to look ahead with excitement and purpose.

We are no longer wishing and wanting but walking in faith.

We are no longer simply surviving but we are planted to flourish wherever the military sends us!

Meet the Contributors

Kelli Baker is a **Staff Writer** for **Planting Roots**. Baker joined the Army at the age of 21 and met her husband while serving at Fort Meade. When they decided to start a family, her uniform and paratrooper boots were tucked away while she cared for their newborn son. She is grateful the military provided the opportunity to earn a Masters of Arts in Organizational Leadership and a Masters of Science in Finance. However, Kelli discovered her true passion for encouraging and inspiring women when she began leading praise and worship at her local Protestant Women of the Chapel. In her free time, Kelli enjoys baking and biking, along with gardening and spending time outdoors with her two children. She dreams of one day authoring her own devotional book, encouraging women to grow in their relationship with the Father.

Claudia Duff is a **Staff Writer** for **Planting Roots**. As a member of the Planting Roots speaking team, she enjoys conducting workshops and speaking at their one-day events around the country. Claudia lives in Virginia with her retired Navy husband. Most days when she's not writing or planning a conference for Planting Roots, you can find her sitting in her sewing chair creating Grammy-made clothing for her GrandDufflings.

Liz Giertz is the **Blog Editor** for **Planting Roots** and an Army veteran who traded her combat boots for a pink ID Card and a craft apron. She, her husband, their two boisterous boys, and one crazy shelter pup call the hills of West Virginia home, at least until her soldier retires from active duty. She is passionate about gathering women around her craft table and encouraging them with God's Word. She also writes at **www.lizgiertz.com** and has published a pair of workbooks aimed at helping military couples reconnect after deployment—*Marriage Maintenance: Tune Up After Time Apart for Him* and *For Her*.

Jillian Gilbey is the **Graphic Designer** for **Planting Roots**. She is an Army wife of twelve years and mom to three children. She is passionate about radically-ordinary, Gospel-centered hospitality, and hopes that the love of God can be poured out within the local community one open door at a time. She desires to serve God through the creative abilities he has blessed her with to one day form a bridge between military and civilian women. It is her prayer that women from all backgrounds can connect on the common ground of faith, community, and grace.

Kristin Goodrich, known as "KG" on the **Planting Roots** team, serves as the **XO** (second in command) to the Director of Planting Roots. She proudly wore a Navy uniform for eight years and has been married to her retired Air Force husband for twenty-five years. She is third-generation Navy and is thankful for the opportunity to raise three kids in the military community. With a tendency to laugh loudly, KG loves to read lots of books, speak in various languages, do fire mitigation, and try new activities such as ballet. She is happy to have put down roots in Colorado.

Muriel Gregory is the **Bible Study Editor** for **Planting Roots** and the author of ***Rise Up: Awaken the Leader Within You***. Currently living in Eastern Kansas, she loves being involved in a discipleship movement for greater Kansas City. Muriel and her active duty Army husband have been married twenty-six years and have three children. Connect with Muriel on Instagram @Muriel.Gregory.

Ginger Harrington is the **Director of Publishing** and **Senior Editor** for **Planting Roots,** as well as serving on the

Speaking Team. A founding member of Planting Roots, she is honored to establish the Planting Roots publishing imprint, a long-term dream of empowering military women to share their stories. Author of the award-winning book, ***Holy in the Moment: Simple Ways to Love God and Enjoy Your Life***, Ginger is blogger, broadcaster, and engaging speaker for military and civilian audiences. Ginger and her retired Marine husband have been married for thirty-one years and have three young adult children. Get free resources to deepen faith from Ginger at **www.Ginger Harrington.com** or connect with her on Facebook or Instagram @GingerHarrington.

Ellie Kay (guest writer) is the founder and CEO of Heroes at Home, a 501(c)(3) that provides financial literacy to our military members. She is the author of fifteen books, is a popular speaker, corporate educator and spokesperson, and mother of five millennial children. Ellie has walked her own financial talk and knows what it's like to be strapped for cash and struggling. She teaches sound money habits that are doable and will stretch a person's dollars for desired lifestyles. One of her latest titles, ***Living Rich for Less*** (Waterbook/Random House, January 2009), sets forth her 10/10/80T Rule—give away 10-percent of your income, save 10-percent, and spend the last 80-percent wisely—with hundreds of Cha-Ching Factor™ tips that show readers how to keep and put more than $30,000 in their pockets in just one year.

Chaplain (Colonel-retired) Art Pace serves as the vice president of the **Board of Directors** for **Planting Roots**. He ministered for thirty years in the Army. After his retirement, he was the executive director of the Armed Services Ministry of **American Bible Society** for three years. He then worked with Wycliffe Associates, The 1687 Foundation, and Olive Branch International. He is currently a part time contractor with the Armed Services Ministry. He is co-author of the books *Engage Your Strengths 4.0* and *The Military Stewardship Devotional*. He's had op-ed pieces published in the *Huffington Post*, *Christian Post*, and the ABS blog site. He has been married to his wife Mary for forty-six years. He has two daughters, Megan and Theresa, and four grandchildren.

Dr. Brenda Pace serves as **Advisor** on the **Planting Roots** staff and **Theological Editor**. With a passion to bring encouragement and hope to women, her journey has taken her from small-town beginnings in Tennessee, around the world as a military wife and back again as an author, speaker, and military ministry consultant. Her most recent book series, ***Journey of a Military Wife, God's Truth for Every Step*** follows the journey of multiple biblical characters and makes application to the modern-day woman. Co-authoring two books with Carol McGlothlin, Brenda's other books include ***The One-Year Yellow Ribbon Devotional: Take a Stand in Prayer for Our Nation and Those Who Serve*** and ***Medals Above My Heart: The Rewards of Being a Military Wife***. Brenda also served eight years on the international board of Protestant Women of the Chapel.

Katye Riselli served three years as **Event Team Lead,** as well as **Writer and Editor** for **Planting Roots**. A known storyteller with a passion for the written word, Katye previously served as Speechwriter and Deputy Communications Director for Mrs. Laura Bush. Since marrying into the military, Katye now uses stories to encourage women to live what they believe by digging deep roots of faith. Katye writes at www.katyeriselli.com about life in the military, rediscovering faith, and building community. Katye and her husband have two daughters and now call Kansas City, Missouri home. When she's not writing, you'll find her chasing her girls or reading a good book. You can connect with her on social media @kdriselli.

Larissa Traquair serves on the **Social Media Team** for **Planting Roots.** A popular broadcaster, Larissa's passion is to help others realize that adopting an attitude of gratitude will make a world of difference in their lives and in the lives of those around them. To accomplish this mission, God called her to broadcast live on various platforms. Known as the GR8TFUL Chick, Chief Inspirational Officer (CIO) of the GR8TFUL Tribe, she impacts many with her vibrant and positive message even in the journey of losing her Marine husband to a long battle with cancer. Connect with Larissa and the GR8TFUL Tribe at www.Gr8tfulChick.com or @gr8tfulchick on Facebook.

Jennifer Wake is a **Staff Writer** for **Planting Roots** and also serves as the **Administration Team Leader**. Jennifer has been a Christian for thirty-plus years and still learning about Christ daily. As the wife of an Army chaplain, Jennifer has been involved in Protestant Women of the Chapel for eighteen years. Jennifer's true passion is to teach and to serve the military community.

Tami Waring served two years as an **Editor** for **Planting Roots** and is the wife of Hous Waring, retired Air Force and currently on staff with Officers' Christian Fellowship. Tami accepted a position with Officers' Christian Fellowship as the Staff Representative for Women's Engagement. A 1984 graduate of the US Air Force Academy who then served five years in Colorado Springs, Tami is the mother of nine children and grandmother to ten—so far. She turned in her uniform for a suitcase and followed Hous around the world.

Rachelle Whitfield is the **Marketing Director** for **Planting Roots**. She is an Army veteran, Army wife, and mom of four boys, two with four paws. She has been a financial counselor in the military community for more than ten years, a residential planner for nearly twenty years, a speaker, and aspiring writer. She is passionate about helping military women create a lifestyle full of "*ABUNDANCE.*" Rachelle loves adventure and travel. She currently resides in North Carolina with her husband Chris and their dogs, Pokey and Jack. They enjoyed overseas tours in Asia with a love of travel. She loves football and is a Cowboy and Missouri Tiger fan until the end. Connect with her on Instagram @rachellesamone.

Courtney Woodruff served one year as the Web Manager for **Planting Roots** and is now a full-time homemaker, blogger, and children's book author. With a heart for foster care, adoptions, and military families, she believes God does amazing things when we bravely share our gifts, skills, and stories with others. Connect with Courtney at www.courtneywoodruff.com.

Kori Yates is the **Director** and **Founder** of **Planting Roots**. Author of ***Olive Drab Pom-Poms***, Kori is a popular speaker and trainer. She writes at **www.KoriYates.com** and has written articles for Officers' Christian Fellowship's *COMMAND* magazine, as well as other publications and blogs. Kori and her active duty Army husband have been married for fourteen years and have two children. To learn more about Kori, visit her website or connect with her on Instagram @korikyates.

ABOUT PLANTING ROOTS

Our **MISSION** is to encourage military women
and wives to grow in their faith.
Our **VISION** is that all military women
and wives will be deeply rooted in Christ.

Who We Are
Planting Roots is an interdenominational Protestant organization of military women and wives. Our heartbeat is to connect, encourage, and equip each other to do what God has called us to in the places we are planted. We believe together we can impact an entire globe for Christ because we truly span the globe from Georgia to Germany, Kansas to Korea, and Alaska to Afghanistan. If we could accomplish this with the estimated 250,000 Bible-believing, Christ-following military women and wives around the world we become one of the greatest missionary movements of our time.

What We Do
Planting Roots has three main focuses: community, resources, and events. Through Planting Roots, the Lord is building a community of Christian military women through social media, online Bible study, local meet ups, and interactive groups. The resources produced are Bible-based resources that speak directly to our military lives with a foundation of the Gospel. Additionally, we host both in-person and virtual events where connection truly comes to life. Here we worship, learn, and grow together.

How You Can Help
Planting Roots stands at the unique intersection of Christian, Military, and Women. You can help by sharing within your sphere of influence about the community here. Also, as a 501c3, donations are also welcome. They can be made via snail mail, our website, or the FREE Planting Roots App.
<u>Mailing address</u>: PO Box 84, Leavenworth, KS 66048

MILITARY. CHRISTIAN. WOMEN

AT PLANTING ROOTS,

we connect with women through

Live Events

Planting Roots hosts annual Strength to Thrive conferences in locations from Germany to San Diego as well as online. These conferences provide connection, encouragement, worship, Jesus, and fun - FOR military women BY military women.

Online Community

With an online community of over 6,000 military women and wives, Planting Roots provides faith-based connections regardless of location. Through live videos, social media posts, and digital communication, women can stay inspired and encouraged together.

Resources

Bible-based resources written specifically by military women for military women is a big part of what we do. We have produced multiple Bible studies and hard copy devotionals, as well as additional resources available online with new materials being produced each year.

Visit our website to learn more!

Don't forget to stop by our online store while you are there. From hats and t-shirts to tote bags and coffee mugs, we have PR swag just for you.

PLANTINGROOTS.NET

OUR RESOURCES

MONDAY

Join us on our blog every Monday as we share Biblical encouragement to grow in our faith throughout our military journeys.

TUESDAY

Every Tuesday morning, Kori shares her heart for God and military wives and women on Facebook Live

WEDNESDAY

Be encouraged by military women just like you on our podcast. A new episode released every other Wednesday.

THURSDAY

Join us live on Instagram every Thursday morning as we pray for our sisters in Christ and our military community.

FRIDAY

On Fridays, we share personal stories of what God has uniquely taught us as we walk through this military life.

ANY TIME

Available on YouTube, this two-week video devotional series is full of Biblical encouragement for every season.

WE HAVE AN APP FOR THAT!

Find all of our resources in the same place with the PR app. Download or get it today:

OUR BIBLE STUDIES

You Have a Place at the Wall
In this six-week study, you will dig deeply into each chapter of the historical book of Nehemiah, finding God's faithfulness on every page and realizing that we all have a place at the wall. You will also examine themes such as prayer, integrity, leadership, justice, and worship. Content and application questions will help you mine the depths of this important book of the Bible.

In Relationship with God
This collaboration between Planting Roots and the American Bible Society was developed specifically for women in uniform. Bible Boot Camp for Military Women is a 45-day devotional that will encourage female service members as they serve both God and their country. Chaplains and pastoral staff can request this resource in bulk orders for chapels and ministries directly from the American Bible Society.

Moments with God
Whether you are a woman in uniform or a military family member, life in the military can be challenging. The Free to Be Brave devotional includes moments with God written by military women for military women. Discover the blessings of living in Christ's freedom to be brave, authentic, grateful, and expectant. Together let's embrace our freedom and enjoy this military life!

Bloom Where You're Planted
The Bible calls us to persevere, but that is easier said than done, especially when life gets tough. How do you persevere when inconsistency is your constant, and your closest friends are thousands of miles away? Growing Together answers that question and more. Using the book of Hebrews as a backdrop, explore issues such as spiritual drifting, encouragement, holding fast, and the need for intentional community.

Flourish Where You're Sent
Based on solid principles from the word of God, Flourish, a study of Psalm 92, teaches: how to show gratitude when all you want to do is complain; how to praise God for who he is, not just what he does; how to spend time in God's presence even when life is hard; and how to love others when military life stresses you out and wears you down. Journey through Psalm 92 and begin to live the flourishing life Jesus promised.

Faith to Stand Firm
Whether you are a seasoned Bible veteran or a new recruit to God's Word, you will learn fresh concepts and God's good plans for you to live in spiritual freedom. With lessons and examples applied to military life, Beyond Brave will show you how to stand firm on God's truth, even in the challenges of military experience. Go beyond the battles you face today and be brave in the good fight of faith.